A History of Desert Tortoise Research at Saguaro National Park

Version 4 (4/6/2009)

Natural Resource Report NPS/SODN/NRR—2009/100

Erin R. Zylstra and Don E. Swann

Saguaro National Park
3693 South Old Spanish Trail
Tucson, Arizona 85730-5601

April 2009

U.S. Department of the Interior
National Park Service
Natural Resource Program Center
Fort Collins, Colorado

The Natural Resource Publication series addresses natural resource topics that are of interest and applicability to a broad readership in the National Park Service and to others in the management of natural resources, including the scientific community, the public, and the NPS conservation and environmental constituencies. Manuscripts are peer-reviewed to ensure that the information is scientifically credible, technically accurate, appropriately written for the intended audience, and is designed and published in a professional manner.

Natural Resource Reports are the designated medium for disseminating high priority, current natural resource management information with managerial application. The series targets a general, diverse audience, and may contain NPS policy considerations or address sensitive issues of management applicability. Examples of the diverse array of reports published in this series include vital signs monitoring plans; monitoring protocols; "how to" resource management papers; proceedings of resource management workshops or conferences; annual reports of resource programs or divisions of the Natural Resource Program Center; resource action plans; fact sheets; and regularly-published newsletters.

Views, statements, findings, conclusions, recommendations and data in this report are solely those of the author(s) and do not necessarily reflect views and policies of the U.S. Department of the Interior, NPS. Mention of trade names or commercial products does not constitute endorsement or recommendation for use by the National Park Service.

Printed copies of reports in these series may be produced in a limited quantity and they are only available as long as the supply lasts. This report is also available from the Sonoran Desert Network, Saguaro National Park, and the Natural Resource Publications Management website (http://www.nature.nps.gov/publications/NRPM) on the Internet.

Please cite this publication as:

Zylstra, E. R., and D. E. Swann. 2009. A history of desert tortoise research at Saguaro National Park. Natural Resource Report NPS/SODN/NRR—2009/100. National Park Service, Fort Collins, Colorado.

NPS D-183, April 2009

Contents

Figures

Executive Summary

Photo by E. Zylstra

Desert tortoises (*Gopherus agassizii*) occur in both the Rincon Mountain District and Tucson Mountain District of Saguaro National Park. Tortoises have been called "walking saguaros" because both are long-lived and found on rocky desert slopes. They are very popular with park visitors. Although tortoises in Arizona are not threatened or endangered (as they are in all other states), they are protected and considered sensitive. Many recent studies in the park have evaluated the natural history and conservation status of the desert tortoise; indeed much of what we know about this species in Arizona is based on studies at the park. This report summarizes the results of these studies in anticipation that this information will be valuable for future research and management of this long-lived animal.

NPS Photos

Although most tortoises in the Sonoran Desert inhabit areas below 1220 m (4000 ft) in elevation, tortoises in Saguaro National Park have been observed well above this elevation. A known population occurs between 1400-1500 m (4600-4900 ft) on the south side of the Rincon Mountains (habitat pictured above left). In 2000, a tortoise was observed near the top of the Rincon Mountains in coniferous forest at 2380 m (7808 ft; pictured above right), which is the highest elevation ever recorded for this species.

Density of desert tortoises (number of adults per unit area) in the Rincon Mountain District are among the highest observed in the Sonoran Desert. Mark-recapture studies were completed at three sites in the Rincon Mountain District and one site in the Tucson Mountain District in the 1980's and 1990's, and distance-sampling studies were completed in both districts between 2000 and 2006. Density estimates in the Rincon Mountain District ranged from 33-52 adult tortoises/km^2(13-20 tortoises/mi^2); density estimates for the Panther Peak area in the Tucson Mountain District were similar to those in the Rincon Mountain District, but were slightly lower for the district as a whole (approximately 25 tortoises/km^2, or 10/mi^2).

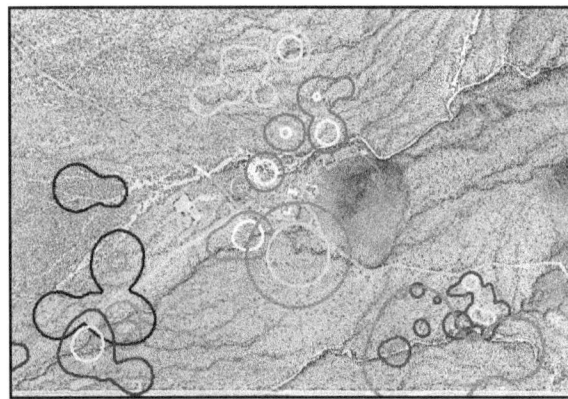

NPS Photo

Numerous radio-telemetry studies at the park have provided information regarding seasonal activity and movement patterns of desert tortoises. The map on the left depicts home ranges of eight adult tortoises near the the Tucson Mountain District Visitor Center between 2006 and 2008. Tortoises generally tend to be faithful to particular areas, often occupying the same shelter-site during consecutive winters. Occasionally however, tortoises will make long-distance movements. One tortoise (nicknamed "Thelma"), first located along the park boundary with the Rocking K Ranch, trekked over 30 km (18.5 miles) south to the Santa Rita Mountains in 2001. She was occasionally aided by people who carried her across human-constructed barriers like I-10 and railroad tracks.

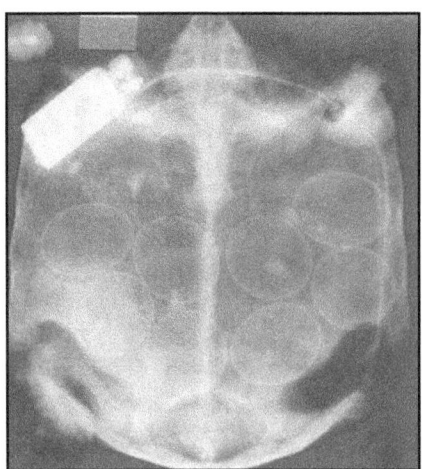

Photo by E. Zylstra

Tortoises are long-lived animals, thought to reach ages of 80-100 years in the wild. Because of their longevity, females usually do not reproduce until they are at least 12-15 years old. Reproductive studies, including one conducted in the Rincon Mountain District between 2000 and 2002, have demonstrated that in the Sonoran Desert, reproduction is closely tied to winter and spring rainfall. Using x-rays and ultrasound, researchers found that females never lay more than one clutch of two to eight eggs in a year, and often wait more than a year between reproductive events.

Photos by E. Zylstra

The diet of desert tortoises varies throughout the year depending on availability of particular plants and seasonal nutritional requirements. Diet studies at the park have used analyses of scat samples and observational bite counts of live tortoises to determine what plants are particularly important to tortoises in this region of the Sonoran Desert. In the spring, tortoises feed primarily on annual legumes, like desert lupine (*Lupinus sparsiflorus*; above right), which contain high amounts of water and low amounts of potassium. When water is available during the summer monsoon season, a typical tortoise diet is composed primarily of annual and perennial grasses, supplemented by prickly pear fruit (*Opuntia engelmannii*) and desert vine (*Janusia gracilis*; above center).

NPS Photo

Blood samples gathered from tortoises in Saguaro National Park were used as part of a regional genetic study between 2000 and 2002. Researchers found only small genetic differences among desert tortoise populations in the Tucson area, suggesting that intermediate gene flow still occurs or occurred until recently among isolated populations, at the rate of ≥ one migrant per generation. Given the increasing number of human-made barriers that will likely prevent future movements between mountain ranges, small tortoise populations undergoing decline may now require occasional augmentation to remain viable.

NPS Photo

Photo by E. Zylstra

Several studies in and near Saguaro National Park have assessed the potential effects of human development along park boundaries on desert tortoise populations. Most of this work has taken place along the south side of the Rincon Mountains, where rapid development is occurring. Baseline data gathered between 1990 and 2005 on population size and home range locations should eventually be useful in providing a picture of the status of this population before and after development.

Photos by E. Zylstra

In areas bordering human development, tortoises may encounter another potential threat from released or abandoned domestic dogs. During desert tortoise surveys completed in the Tucson Mountain District in 2006, researchers noted that an alarming number of tortoises had injuries consistent with attacks by dogs, particularly along park borders. A smaller proportion of tortoises in the Rincon Mountain District presented these injuries, likely because much of the Rincon Mountain District is bordered by protected lands without human development. Injuries sustained by adult tortoises are severe and can impact a tortoise's chances for survival and for successful mating. Although adult tortoises can sometimes survive these brutal attacks, juvenile tortoises likely die as a result.

Photo by E. Zylstra   NPS Photo

Although historically fires were not common at lower elevations in the Sonoran Desert, they are increasing in frequency in recent years due to non-native plants like African buffelgrass *(Pennisetum ciliare)* and red brome *(Bromus rubens)*. In 1994, the Mother's Day Fire was ignited along the east side of the Cactus Forest Loop Road, burning 840 acres (340 hectares) of Arizona Upland desertscrub that tortoises are known to inhabit. Within two months of the fire, mortality surveys were initiated throughout burned areas. Seven tortoise carcasses were found and an estimated 11% of adult tortoises in the area died as a result of the fire. Additional surveys and radio-telemetry studies were conducted in the area for several years following the fire, but did not find significant long-term effects of the fire on the tortoise population.

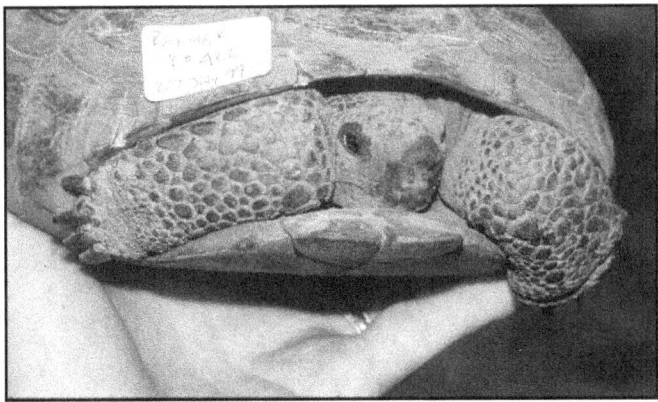

Photo by R. Averill-Murray

Disease, particularly upper respiratory tract disease (URTD), is considered to be one of the primary causes of observed declines in tortoise populations in the Mojave Desert. Although present in the Sonoran Desert, URTD has not been implicated in significant population declines. In 2000 and 2001, 85% of tortoises tested in and near the park tested positive for exposure to URTD. Between 2003 and 2005, samples were collected from tortoises throughout Saguaro

National Park and the greater Tucson area to assess the prevalence of URTD in wild and captive tortoise populations. Over 50% of wild tortoises tested positive for previous exposure to the disease, and over 25% showed signs of current infection, including discharge from the eyes and nose similar to the tortoise pictured above. The good news, however, is that tortoises in the Sonoran Desert appear to be able to clear the infection, having clinical signs one year and not the next.

Photo by E. Zylstra   Photo by D. Prival   Photo by D. Caldwell

The question of how to monitor tortoise populations in the Sonoran Desert has also been addressed by several studies in the park. Mark-recapture methods were used in 1996 and 1997 to estimate tortoise density on long-term monitoring plots. Since then, other methods have been tested, including distance sampling transects to estimate density and repeated presence-absence surveys to estimate what percentage of the park is occupied by tortoises. While a conclusive answer has not yet been reached, survey results from Saguaro National Park have greatly contributed to the discussion.

NPS Photo

During the past several years, park staff have developed a program to bring small groups of high school students out to the park and track radio-marked desert tortoises. In addition to tracking tortoises, the students collect data on weather, tortoise activity, movements, and habitat use. The program provides younger students with an opportunity to learn about the desert and its wildlife and gain hands-on experience using current research techniques in the field. This program has been conducted in concert with research studies, which has improved not only the park's ability to understand tortoises, but to actively conserve them as well.

Acknowledgements

We wish to acknowledge the many researchers, students, and volunteers who conducted tortoise research in the park over the years. Cecil Schwalbe has been instrumental in much of this work, and deserves special credit for his enthusiasm, commitment and vision. Many people helped to assemble the data used in this report, including Pam Anning, Kristen Beaupre, and Josh Capps. Alice Perger and Louise Conrad did a huge amount of copying and data entry for this project, and we are grateful for all their work. We appreciate helpful reviews of this manuscript by Roy Averill-Murray, Taylor Edwards, Andy Hubbard, Cristina Jones, and Meg Weesner.

Desert tortoise research at at Saguaro National Park has been supported by a large number of institutions, including the National Park Service, Arizona Game and Fish Department, University of Arizona, U.S. Geological Survey, Smithsonian Institute, Western National Parks and Monuments Association, Friends of Saguaro National Park, Desert Southwest Cooperative Ecosystems Studies Unit, T&E Inc., Rincon Institute, the Arizona-Sonora Desert Museum, the Rocking K Ranch, Earth Friends Wildlife Foundation, and Beth Spiva Timmons Foundation. In particular, we are grateful to the Western National Parks Association and the Friends of Saguaro National Park for their unflagging support of long-term monitoring and education at Saguaro National Park.

Introduction

Research on the desert tortoise (*Gopherus agassizii*) has taken place at Saguaro National Park since the 1980s. Indeed, it is probably not an exaggeration to say that much of what we know about this species in the Sonoran Desert is the result of research at the park, although other prominent tortoise study sites include the Four Peaks and Sugarloaf Mountain area near Phoenix and Ironwood National Monument northwest of Tucson.

Desert tortoises are found throughout the Mojave and Sonoran Deserts of the United States and Mexico (Germano et al. 1994, Van Devender 2002, Stebbins, 2003). In the Sonoran Desert, tortoises are typically found on rocky hillsides, mountain foothills, and incised washes, and only found in low densities in valley bottoms (Barrett 1990, Germano et al. 1994, Averill-Murray and Averill-Murray 2005). Desert tortoises are found in both districts of the park (Figs. 1 and 2), and although most tortoises in Arizona inhabit areas below 1220 m (4000 ft) in elevation, tortoises have been observed well above this elevation at Saguaro National Park. A known population occurs between 1400-1500 m (4600-4900 ft) along the Chimenea drainage on the south side of the Rincon Mountains (to be discussed later), and in 2000, a single tortoise was observed near the top of the Rincons in coniferous forest at 2380 m (7808 ft), an elevation record for the species (Aslan et al. 2003). We are not aware of any records from the east slope of the Rincons.

Most of the prominent researchers of Sonoran desert tortoises have worked in some capacity at the park, including Roy Averill-Murray and Tom Van Devender; Charles Lowe and his students Peter Holm, Brent Martin, and Elizabeth Wirt; Cecil Schwalbe and his students Taylor Edwards, Cristina Jones, and Eric Stitt; Bob Steidl and his student Erin Zylstra; and prominent Mojave Desert tortoise researchers Todd Esque and Olav Oftedal. Quite a bit of this research is summarized in the book, *The Sonoran Desert Tortoise* (Van Devender 2002). There have also been a large number of published research papers and reports on tortoise research in Saguaro National Park (see below).

Research at Saguaro National Park has provided information on Sonoran Desert tortoise abundance, habitat, distribution, diet, reproduction, genetics, disease, and monitoring strategies. The goal of this short paper is to summarize these studies and their results, and to provide a bibliography of desert tortoise research in the park to date.

Methods

The large amount of research on tortoises at Saguaro National Park led to an effort by park biologists, beginning in the late 1990s, to summarize the data from all of these studies. We made an effort to locate copies of all data sheets, particularly processing data sheets, and records for all marked tortoises at Saguaro National Park. These sheets were copied and – thanks to many students and volunteers – entered into a database that has also been checked and updated regularly. We were not able to get copies of data from every study conducted since the early 1980s, but we were able to obtain a great deal of information. All available copies of processing data sheets are filed, by project and by tortoise number, in the Resource Management office at

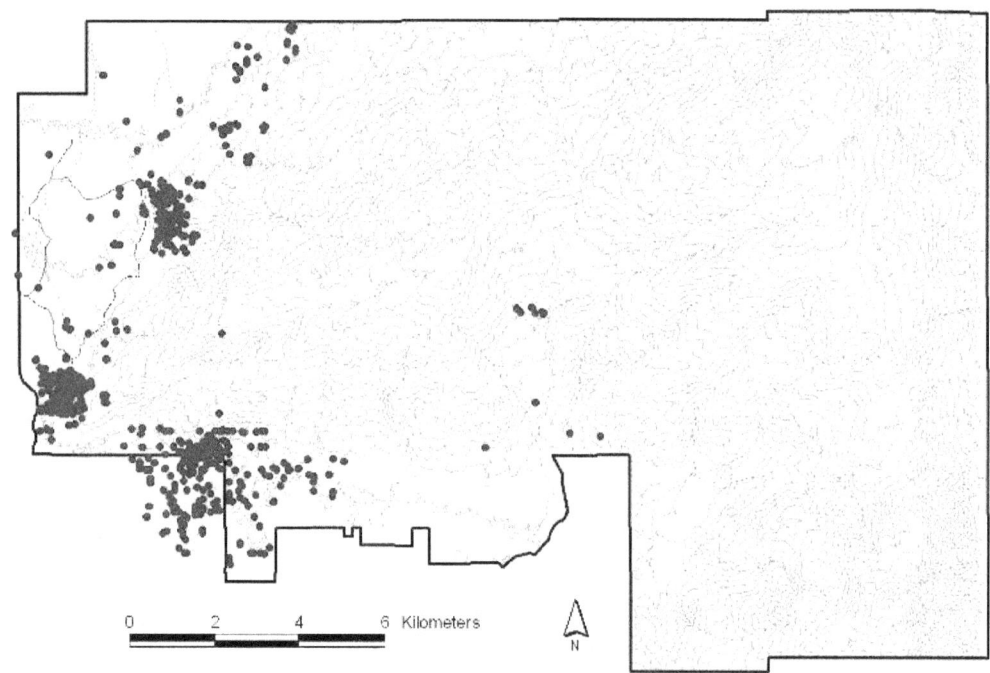

Figure 1. Distribution of desert tortoise observations in and near Saguaro National Park, Rincon Mountain District, 1998-2008. Source: Saguaro National Park files.

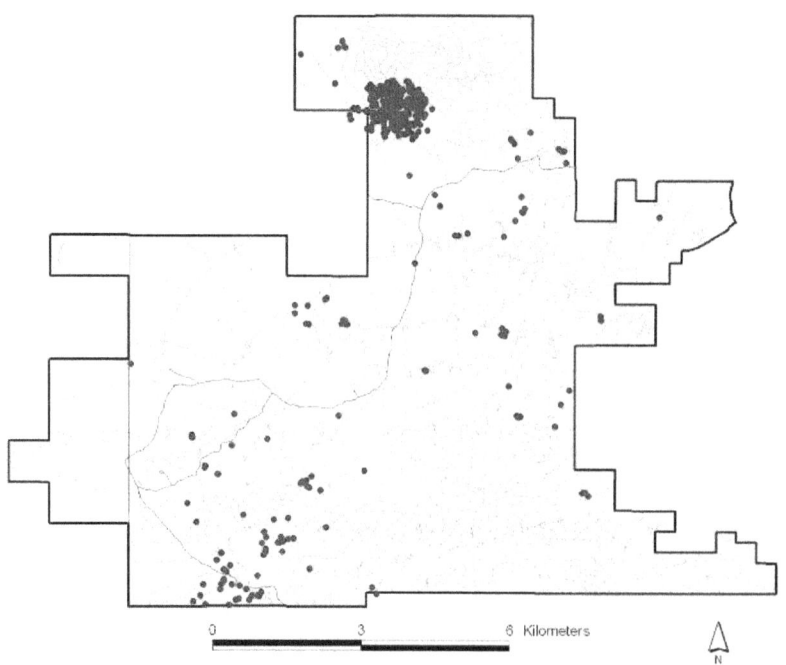

Figure 2. Distribution of desert tortoise observations in Saguaro National Park, Tucson Mountain District, 1998-2008. Source: Saguaro National Park files.

the Rincon Mountain District and have been archived at the Western Archaeological and Conservation Center in Tucson. A database containing information on all documented observations of marked tortoises at Saguaro National Park is located on the park server: N:\GPS\GIS_Work\Tortoise\Marked_Tortoises\Master_GOAG.xls.

Study locations and marking methods

There have been three park-wide studies that have sampled tortoises throughout both the Rincon Mountain District and the Tucson Mountain District. The first study was completed by Audrey Goldsmith in 1988, the second by Betsy Wirt in 1995, and the third by Erin Zylstra in 2005-2006. Other desert tortoise studies have taken place in several established study areas. These include, in the Rincon Mountain District, the Javelina Picnic Area plot, Mother's Day Fire plot, the Rocking K Ranch-Saguaro National Park Expansion area, and the Chimenea area along the Manning Camp trail (Fig. 3). At the Tucson Mountain District, established study sites include the Panther Peak plot and Red Hills/Visitor Center area (Fig. 4).

Hundreds of tortoises in Saguaro National Park have been marked by researchers since the 1980s. Two types of marks have been used: scute notches, and labels. The two types of marks are not mutually exclusive, in fact most tortoises in the park have been marked with both notches and labels. Scute notches are small v-shaped indentations, approximately 0.5 cm (0.2 in) in length and width, permanently filed into the marginal scutes. Eleven marginal scutes are located on each side of the tortoise. Each marginal scute is assigned a unique number within a notching system. A tortoise can be identified by adding up the numbers assigned to each marginal scute that has been notched. Three different notching systems have been used in Saguaro National Park (App. B). The "Wirt" system is now used throughout the park, except on the south side of the Rincon Mountains in the Rocking K Ranch-Saguaro National Park Expansion area. The "Arizona" system has only been used in the Rocking K Ranch-Saguaro National Park Expansion area. Finally, the "Cagle 1939" system was only used briefly between 1994 and 1995 in the Mother's Day Fire area. Most tortoises in the park have also been marked with labels, which are small written numbers affixed to the rear of the carapace with clear epoxy. The benefit of labels is that in many cases a tortoise can be identified without having to handle it or remove it from a shelter-site. Labels typically last about 5-10 years before falling off the carapace. All tortoises in the Saguaro National Park desert tortoise database are identified by both their number and the notching system used to mark them, if applicable.

Results

Goldsmith-Shaw population studies, 1988-1990

The earliest known studies of desert tortoises in Saguaro National Park were initiated in the 1980s as part of a comprehensive effort to study the effects of urban development on wildlife (Shaw et al. 1987). Professor William Shaw in the School of Natural Resources at the University of Arizona collaborated on parts of the project related to desert tortoises with a graduate student, Audrey Goldsmith. As part of the "Relationships between adjacent land uses and the wildlife resources of Saguaro National Monument" project, Goldsmith and Shaw surveyed transects

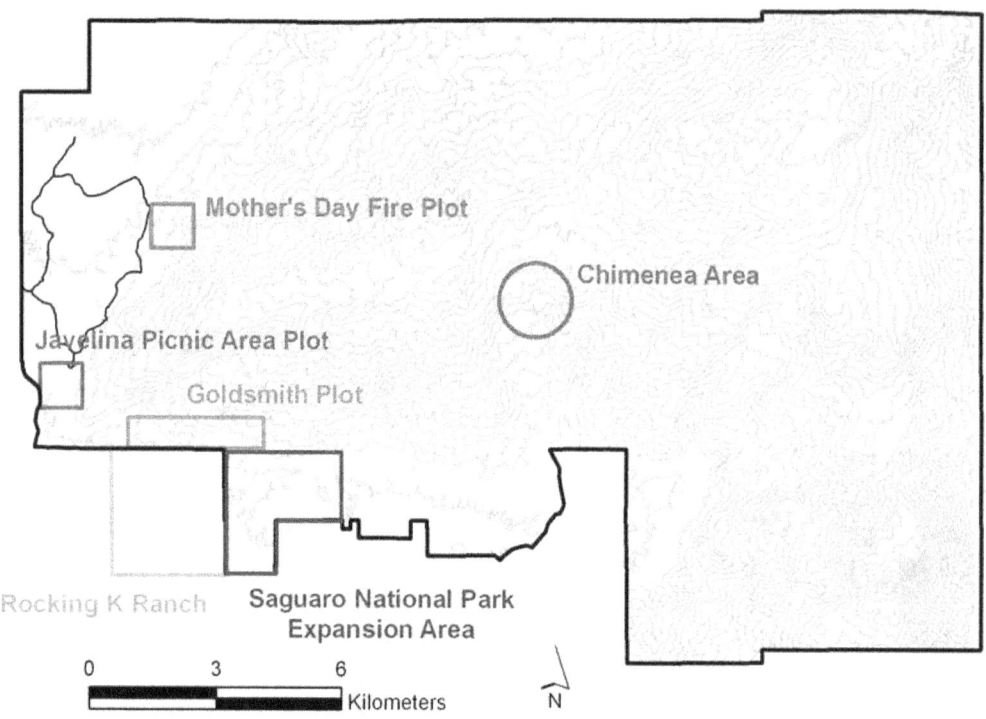

Figure 3. Locations of long-term study areas for desert tortoises in Saguaro National Park, Rincon Mountain District, 1988-2007.

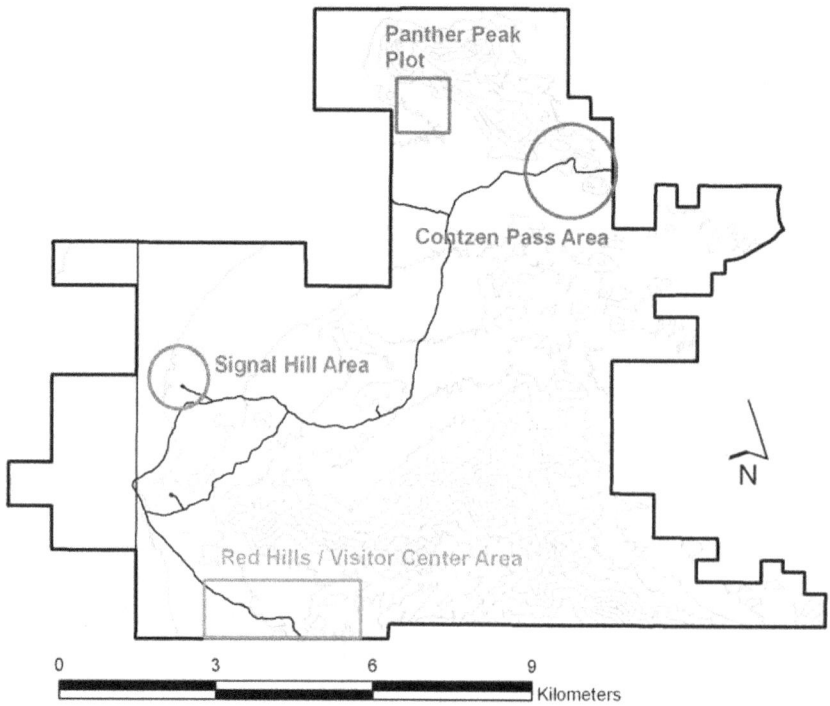

Figure 4. Locations of long-term study areas for desert tortoises in Saguaro National Park, Tucson Mountain District, 1988-2007.

throughout desert tortoise habitat in both districts of the park, completed population surveys at two long-term monitoring plots in the Rincon Mountain District, and tracked radio-marked tortoises at both the Rincon Mountain District and the Tucson Mountain District (Shaw and Goldsmith 1988, Goldsmith and Shaw 1990, Wirt and Robichaux 2001). Although results of many of these studies were never provided to the park due to a serious illness of Audrey Goldsmith, much of the original data was supplied to the park many years later.

In 1988, 14 transects in the Rincon Mountain District and 18 transects in the Tucson Mountain District were surveyed for live tortoises and tortoise sign (scat or carcasses) by Brent Martin, Audrey Goldsmith, and others. Transects in the Rincon Mountain District were primarily located in the western portion of the district, with two located near the Chimenea, Madrona, and Rincon Creek drainages (Fig. 5). Transects in the Tucson Mountain District were located throughout the district (Fig. 6). A report detailing the results of the surveys was never completed by Goldsmith and Shaw, but a summary of their findings was provided several years later in a report submitted to the park by Wirt and Robichaux (2001). During the 1988 surveys, live tortoises or tortoise sign were found on 13/14 transects in the Rincon Mountain District and 11/18 transects in the Tucson Mountain District. They found 18 live tortoises on 11/14 transects in the Rincon Mountain District and 19 tortoises on 9/18 transects in the Tucson Mountain District, and concluded that most areas below 1220 m (4,000 ft) in Saguaro National Park could be considered desert tortoise habitat.

Goldsmith and Shaw completed intensive population surveys of two 2.6 km^2 (1-mi^2) plots in the Rincon Mountain District. In 1989 they hired Brent Martin to survey an area on the northwest side of Tanque Verde Ridge in the Javelina Picnic Area (referred to as the Javelina Picnic Area plot; Fig. 3), and in 1990 they hired Ric Bieser, Nancy Fergusen, and others to survey an area along the southern park boundary adjacent to the Rocking K ranch (Rocking K or Goldsmith plot; Fig. 3). They captured 45 tortoises at the Javelina Picnic Area plot and 32 tortoises at the Rocking K plot (Wirt and Robichaux 2001). Population estimates were not provided to the park, but datasheets associated with each tortoise observation were obtained at a later date.

Finally, in an attempt to estimate home range size and describe movements and seasonal activity patterns of desert tortoises, Goldsmith and Shaw attached radio-transmitters to nine tortoises in the Javelina Picnic Area and four tortoises in the Red Hills area in the Tucson Mountain District in 1988 and 1989. They found that home range sizes, measured by maximum length of the polygons, averaged over 1342 ft (400 m) long, but ranged from 443 ft (135 m) to almost one km (0.62 mi), similar to home range sizes documented for tortoises in the Picacho Peak area (Vaughan 1984, Goldsmith and Shaw 1990).

Van Devender diet study, 1991-1992

In 1991 and 1992, Thomas Van Devender, scientist at the Arizona-Sonora Desert Museum, and colleagues collected fecal samples of desert tortoises from the Tucson Mountains to assess tortoise diet in Arizona Upland habitat. Samples were collected near Contzen Pass and Signal Hill in the Tucson Mountain District (Fig. 4), and Brown Mountain in Tucson Mountain Park, just south of the Tucson Mountain District. They sorted fecal pellets by hand, separated

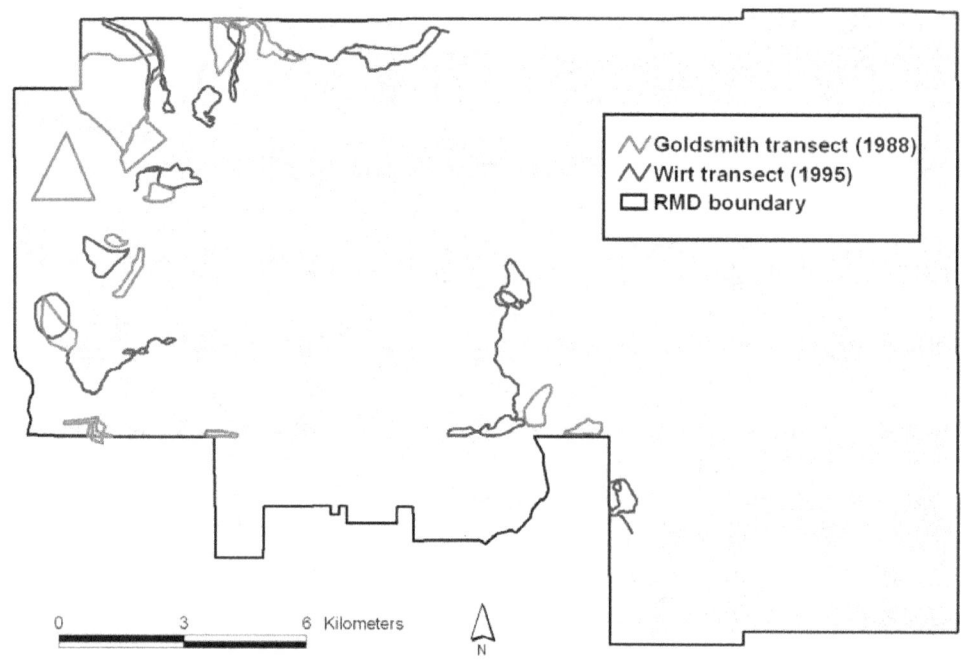

Figure 5. Transects surveyed for desert tortoises in Saguaro National Park, Rincon Mountain District (RMD), 1988-1995.

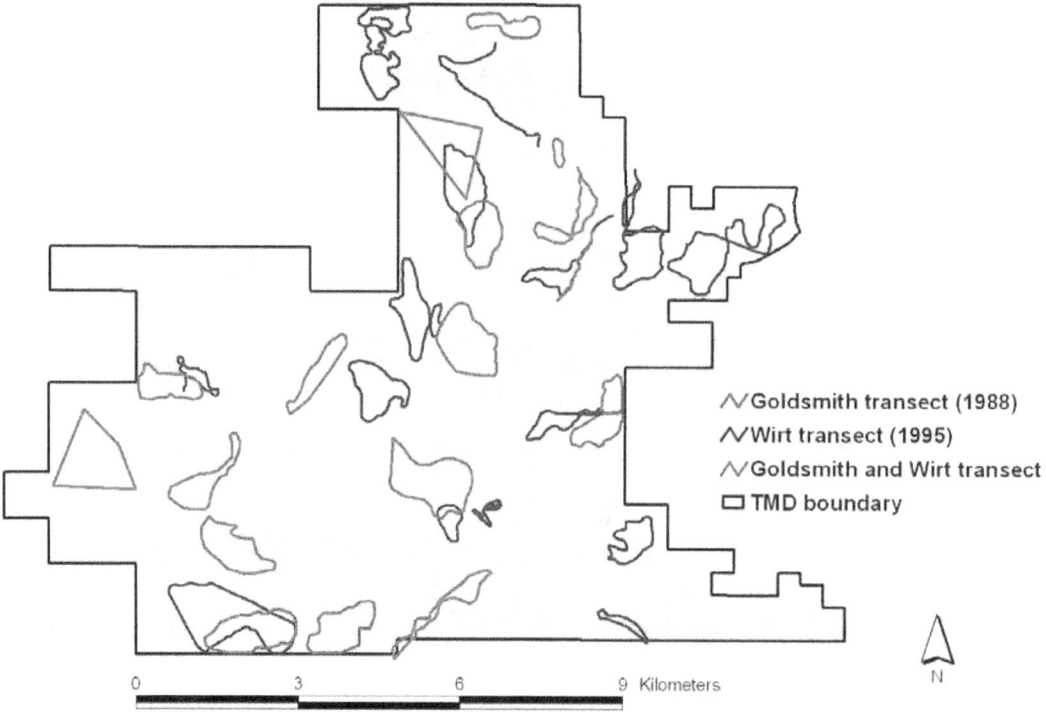

Figure 6. Transects surveyed for desert tortoises in Saguaro National Park, Tucson Mountain District (TMD), 1988-1995.

identifiable plant fragments, and estimated the relative abundance of different plant taxa. They also ground up samples from the Brown Mountain area and subjected the samples to microhistological analyses, in which they identified particular plant taxa by their epidermal characters.

Results from the fragment analysis suggested that grasses were most frequently consumed, although there was a high diversity of annual plants found in the fecal samples. Limited microhistological analyses found high densities of herbaceous perennials, such as *Abutilon* sp. and *Herissantia* sp. (both in the Mallow family) in the fecal samples. Details of the study provided to the park were limited, but can be found in Van Devender and Lawler (1995).

Esque-Schwalbe fire ecology study, 1994-1999

In May 1994, a fire burned approximately 138 ha (340 acres) of Arizona Upland desertscrub east of the Cactus Forest Loop Road in the Rincon Mountain District (Esque et al. 2004; Fig. 3). Within two months of the fire, Todd Esque and Cecil Schwalbe, U.S. Geological Survey scientists with extensive experience studying tortoises in both the Sonoran and Mojave deserts, initiated a study evaluating the effects of fire on saguaros and desert tortoises (Esque et al. 1994). Esque and Schwalbe worked with a number of collaborators and students at the University of Arizona on the Mother's Day Fire project between 1994 and 1999.

In June 1994, Esque and Schwalbe used 10-m (33 ft) wide belt transects to survey the entire area burned within Arizona Upland habitat for desert tortoises. They found six live tortoises and seven carcasses, five of which could be directly attributed to fire, and estimated that approximately 11% of the adult tortoises in the area died (Esque et al. 2003). In 1996, Esque and Schwalbe also attached radio-transmitters to 12 tortoises, six in burned areas and six in unburned areas to assess how tortoises were using these areas. Tortoises were tracked throughout the year, but no differences in movement or activity patterns between tortoises in burned and unburned areas nor long-term effects of the fire on surviving tortoises were observed (C. Schwalbe, personal communication). While not all the data from this study were provided to the park, a summary of the mortality surveys can be found in Esque et al. (2003) and an overview of fire in Arizona Upland habitat, using the Mother's Day Fire as a case study can be found in Esque et al. (2002).

In 1999, Esque and Schwalbe turned over the radio-telemetry study in the Mother's Day Fire area to park biologist Don Swann, who continued monitoring tortoises with the help of Dr. Schwalbe's graduate students and lab technicians at the University of Arizona. Beginning in 1999, Erin Zylstra, Cristina Jones, and several Saguaro National Park volunteers and interns regularly tracked radio-marked tortoises, as often as twice a week during the active season. Radio-telemetry data from the Mother's Day Fire area were incorporated into a number of subsequent desert tortoise studies in the park, including work done by Taylor Edwards, Eric Stitt, Cristina Jones, and Erin Zylstra. Radio-telemetry was discontinued at this site in the spring of 2006, when construction on the Cactus Forest Loop Road prevented access to the site during the upcoming monsoon season.

Wirt-Lowe population studies, 1995-1998

Elizabeth Wirt, a student of Professor Charles Lowe in the Department of Ecology and Evolutionary Biology at the University of Arizona, began desert tortoise studies at the park in 1995. She was assisted by Peter Holm, Steve Hale, and Brett Martin, another Lowe student who studied desert tortoises in the Tortilita Mountains as part of his Master's research project.

Wirt was involved in many desert tortoise projects at Saguaro National Park. She helped to survey for tortoise sign on transects scattered throughout both districts of the park, complete population surveys of several long-term monitoring plots, and track movements of radio-marked tortoises at the Mother's Day Fire site and a high elevation site near the Chimenea drainage along the Manning Camp trail. Wirt summarized these studies in an unpublished report (Wirt and Robichaux 2001) and provided copies of her original data sheets to the park.

In 1995, Wirt and colleagues surveyed 13 transects in the Rincon Mountain District and 18 transects in the Tucson Mountain District for live tortoises and tortoise sign (Figs. 5 and 6). Many transects overlapped considerably with transects surveyed by Goldsmith and Shaw in 1988. Live tortoises or tortoise sign were found on all transects in the Rincon Mountain District and 9/18 transects in the Tucson Mountain District. They found 16 tortoises on 8/13 transects in the Rincon Mountain District and nine tortoises on 4/18 transects in the Tucson Mountain District. Although fewer adult tortoises were found in 1995 despite increased efforts (person hours), differences in encounter rates between the two studies were not significant.

Four tortoises, two males and two females, were found during a transect survey in 1995 along Chimenea Canyon between 1400-1500 m (4600-4900 ft) and were subsequently fitted with radio-transmitters (Fig. 3) because they were some of the highest elevation tortoises known from this region of the Sonoran Desert. The area can be described primarily as semi-desert grassland, with patches of madrean evergreen woodland along riparian areas. Tortoises were tracked between October 1995 and April 1998. Movement patterns of these high-elevation tortoises did not appear to differ considerably from lower-elevation tortoises.

Wirt and colleagues also completed intensive mark-recapture surveys at three 1-km^2 (0.39 mi^2) monitoring plots in the park. In 1996, the Javelina Picnic Area plot (reconfigured and reduced in size from the 1989 survey) and Mother's Day Fire plot in the Rincon Mountain District (Fig. 3) and the Panther Peak plot in the Tucson Mountain District (Fig. 4) were surveyed. In 1997, the Javelina Picnic Area and Panther Peak plots were resurveyed. Density estimates ranged from 39-49 adult tortoises/km^2 (15-19 mi^2) at the Javelina Picnic Area and Panther Peak plots during the two years of surveys, some of the highest tortoise densities reported in the Sonoran Desert (Averill-Murray et al. 2002). Estimated tortoise density at the Mother's Day site (33 adults/km^2, or 12.7/mi^2) was lower than densities at the other two sites, but encouraging given that the area burned only two years before.

Urban impact studies, 1999-2001

In 1999, several studies were initiated in the Rocking K-Saguaro National Park Expansion area to evaluate the long-term effects of land use change on desert tortoise populations along the park's southern boundary (Fig. 3). These studies were done in collaboration with scientists from the University of Arizona (Cecil Schwalbe, Taylor Edwards, and others), the Arizona Game and Fish Department (Roy Averill-Murray), Saguaro National Park (Don Swann), and the Rincon Institute, with support from the Rocking K Ranch. The studies initiated in 1999 were an expansion of an earlier collaboration in 1994-1995 that collected baseline data on the reptile and amphibian species found in the Rincon Valley and bordering Saguaro National Park Expansion area (Murray 1995, Murray 1996), as well as data on birds, plants, and mammals.

Beginning in July 1999, radio-transmitters were attached to tortoises on both sides of the park boundary with the Rocking K Ranch. The study was designed to investigate changes in habitat use, activity, and movements as a result of development in the Rincon Valley. Home range estimates for tortoises along the park border averaged 10.2 ha (25 ha; 95% CI = 5.8-18.0) based on minimum convex polygons [MCP]), and did not differ significantly from estimates for tortoises in the Mother's Day Fire area between 1999 and 2001 (Schwalbe et al. 2002). Project collaborators continued to track tortoises until radios were removed in spring of 2005, and the data were used in several studies carried out by Cecil Schwalbe's graduate students, described below. Although the study was originally designed to look at differences in tortoise populations before and after development, as of this writing in 2009, the ranch has still not been developed.

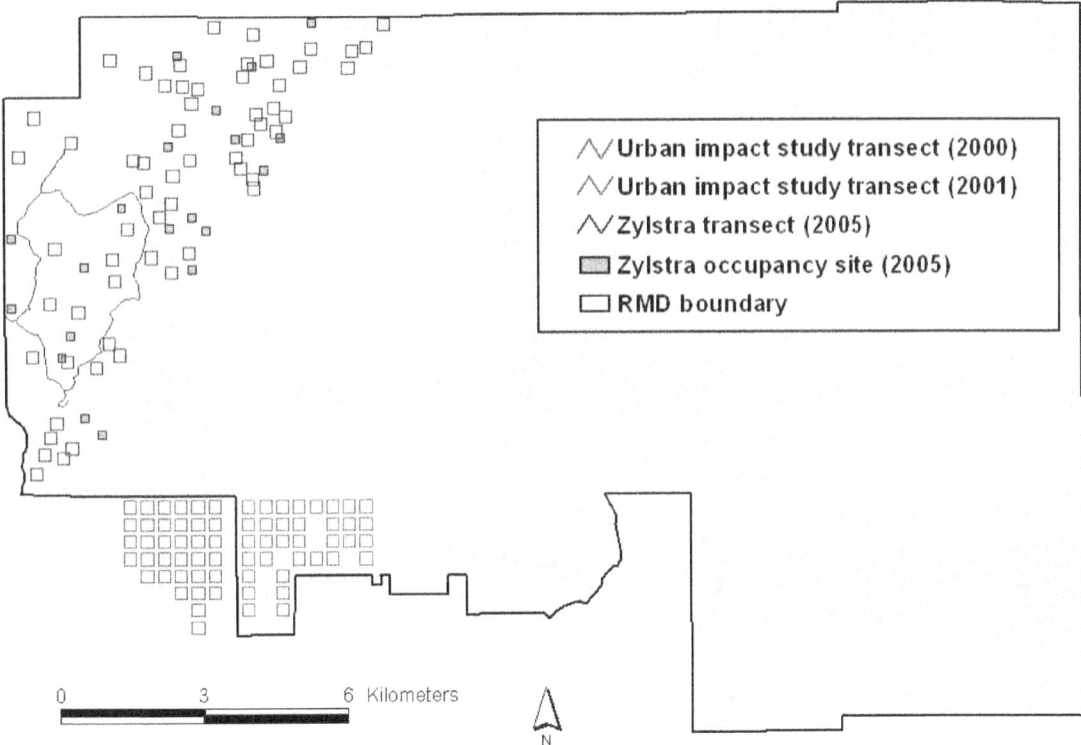

Figure 7. Distance-sampling transects and occupancy sites surveyed for desert tortoises in and near Saguaro National Park, Rincon Mountain District (RMD), 2000-2005.

During the course of the radio-telemetry project, researchers documented an extraordinary long-distance movement by an adult female tortoise originally marked and fitted with a radio-

9

transmitter just south of the park border. Over the course of one year, the tortoise, nicknamed "Thelma," moved more than a 30-km (18.5 mi) straight-line distance from the Rincon Mountains to the Santa Rita Mountains (occasionally aided across human-made barriers; Edwards et al. 2004b). After the tortoise was found between the two mountain ranges near I-10 the next year, researchers moved the tortoise back to its original capture location in the Saguaro National Park Expansion area. Although biologists have previously noted that tortoises are likely to make long-distance movements, documentation of such an extreme movement is very rare.

As part of this study in 2000 and 2001, project collaborators used distance sampling to estimate the number of tortoises on the Rocking K Ranch and the Saguaro National Park Expansion area. Around this time, researchers were investigating how to implement distance-sampling methods as part of a long-term monitoring strategy for tortoises in the Mojave Desert (Anderson et al. 2001, U.S. Fish and Wildlife Service 2006). This study represents the first attempt to use distance-sampling methods to estimate density of tortoises in the Sonoran Desert. With the help of many student interns and volunteers, 34 1-km (3281 ft) transects on the Rocking K Ranch were each surveyed twice in 2000 and 34 1-km transects in the Saguaro National Park Expansion area were each surveyed twice in 2001 (Fig. 7). Don Swann, Roy Averill-Murray with the Arizona Game and Fish Department, and Cecil Schwalbe estimated density of adult tortoises to be $52/km^2$ ($20/mi^2$)in the Rocking K Ranch (Swann et al. 2001, Swann et al. 2002) and $41/km^2$ ($15.8/mi^2$) in the Saguaro National Park Expansion area (Averill-Murray and Swann 2002). Density estimates from the distance-sampling study were similar to those generated using mark-recapture methods on long-term monitoring plots in 1996 and 1997 (Wirt and Robichaux 2001). Data sheets and results from these studies were provided to the park in Swann et al. (2001) and Averill-Murray and Swann (2002). Results from 2000 were also published in the Journal of Wildlife Management (Swann et al. 2002).

Edwards-Schwalbe genetics study, 2000-2002

Taylor Edwards, a graduate student of Cecil Schwalbe and Saguaro National Park volunteer, initiated the first study of desert tortoise genetics at the park in 2000. The goal of the study was to determine if historical movements occurred between what are now isolated populations of desert tortoises in the mountain ranges surrounding Tucson. Edwards studied populations of tortoises in the Rincon Mountain District, the Tucson Mountain District, Desert Peak area, Florence area, Picacho Mountains, Ragged Top Mountain, Sugarloaf Mountain, Tumamoc Hill, and the West Silver Bell Mountains. In addition, an evaluation of genetic relatedness among individuals was completed for tortoises in the Rincon Mountain District, because supplementary information regarding movement and home range sizes was available through on-going radio-telemetry studies.

After developing PCR primers for six microsatellite loci, Edwards and his colleagues found that there were minimal genetic differences among desert tortoise populations in the Tucson area (Edwards et al. 2003, Edwards et al. 2004a). This suggested that intermediate gene flow still occurs or occurred until recently among isolated populations, at the rate of $\geq$ one migrant per generation. Given the proliferation of anthropogenic barriers that will likely prevent future movements between mountain ranges, small tortoise populations may now require occasional augmentation to remain viable. After the project was completed, all original data sheets were provided to the park and results from the study were provided in a report (Edwards et al. 2002), in Edwards's thesis (Edwards 2003), and published in the journal, Conservation Genetics (Edwards et al. 2004a).

Genetic data gathered by Edwards in Saguaro National Park in 2000-2001 are also contributing to long-term research evaluating relationships among desert tortoises throughout their range. Recent work suggests that tortoises in the Mojave and Sonoran deserts have not exchanged genetic material in more than four million years, strengthening the case being made by some that Sonoran and Mojave tortoises represent separate species (Murphy et al. 2007). Additionally, comparisons between samples collected in the Mojave and northern Sonoran deserts, including the Rincon Mountain District, and samples recently gathered in southern Sonora, Mexico indicate that tortoises at the southern extent of their range differ considerably from those in and near the United States (T. Edwards, personal communication).

Stitt-Schwalbe ecology and reproduction study, 2000-2002

Eric Stitt, another graduate student of Cecil Schwalbe and Saguaro National Park volunteer, initiated a number of desert tortoise studies at both the Mother's Day Fire area and Rocking K Ranch-Saguaro National Park Expansion area between 2000 and 2002. Radio-telemetry data gathered at the Rocking K site were used to characterize home range size and movements of tortoises prior to development at the Rocking K Ranch. Stitt worked closely with Roy Averill-Murray from the Arizona Game and Fish Department, using x-ray and ultrasound to describe patterns of reproduction in tortoises at both study sites. Additionally, an undergraduate biology student at the University of Arizona, Amber Blythe, worked with Stitt to complete field experiments evaluating the effects of small-scale translocation on desert tortoises.

Mean yearly home range size (MCP) for tortoises at both study sites was 15.7 ha (39 acres; Stitt et al. 2003c), somewhat larger than the estimate provided by Schwalbe et al. (2002). This difference may be due to several tortoises that made long-distance movements in the Rocking K area in 2002. Home range sizes did not differ between the two sites or between males and females, although males did tend to have slightly larger home ranges. Stitt's data on tortoise reproduction corroborated results from one of Roy Averill-Murray's earlier studies (Averill-Murray 2002), which indicated that unlike tortoises in the Mojave Desert, Sonoran desert tortoises never lay more than one clutch in a year. Additionally, both the number of eggs laid and the number of females laying eggs in a given year were correlated with the amount of winter and spring rainfall (Stitt et al. 2003c). Finally, the distance tortoises were translocated affected movement patterns. Many individuals returned to their original locations within two or three days after they were translocated 800 m (2625 ft), suggesting that while small-scale translocations may not have a negative effect on the tortoise, they also may not prevent tortoises from returning to areas where they were translocated from. Original data sheets from all tortoises handled during the project were not available, but a detailed summary of results was provided in a report to the park and in Stitt's thesis (Stitt et al. 2003; Stitt 2004). Additionally, as part of these research projects, short reports were produced documenting the use of infrared cameras to monitor nest survival and burrow associates of tortoises (Stitt et al. 2003a), Gila monster predation of tortoise nests (Stitt et al. 2003b), tortoise association with Africanized bees (Stitt et al. 2005), and tortoise caliche mining (Stitt and Davis 2003).

Oftedal nutritional ecology study, 2003-2004

Olav Oftedal, a biologist with the Smithsonian Institution, incorporated data collected in the Mother's Day Fire area in 2003-2004 into part of a larger study evaluating spring and summer foraging behavior of tortoises in the Sonoran Desert. In August 2003, Oftedal, along with Smithsonian staff and park volunteers, observed 11 tortoises foraging for a total of 118 hours and catalogued the number of bites taken of each plant species eaten. They completed similar work in April 2004, observing five tortoises for a total of 55 hours. Similar spring and summer observations were completed at Ragged Top, in the Ironwood Forest National Monument and Sugarloaf Mountain in the Tonto National Forest between 2002 and 2004.

In the spring, tortoises selected plants with high water and protein contents and low potassium contents. In the Mother's Day Fire area, more than half of tortoises' diets in the spring consisted of annual legumes, including *Lotus humistratus* (spreading lotus), *Lupinus sparsiflorus* (desert lupine), and *Astragalus nuttallianus* (Nuttal's milkvetch). Tortoises were less selective during the summer, eating mostly annual and perennial grasses, including *Bouteloua aristidoides* (needle grama) and *Panicum* sp. (panic grass). Additionally, tortoises favored *Janusia gracilis* (desert vine) in both the spring and summer and *Opuntia engelmannii* (prickly pear) fruit when ripe in the summer. For additional results from this nutritional ecology study, see Oftedal (2007).

Jones-Schwalbe disease study, 2003-2005

Another Schwalbe graduate student, Cristina Jones, studied desert tortoises in Saguaro National Park and the greater Tucson area to evaluate patterns of disease occurrence and effects of upper respiratory tract disease (URTD) on home range size and winter temperature selection. Disease, particularly URTD, is considered to be one of the primary causes of observed declines in Mojave desert tortoise populations (Knowles 1989, Jacobson et al. 1991, USFWS 1994). Although present in the Sonoran Desert, URTD has not been implicated in significant population declines. An alarming number of tortoises in the Rincon Mountain District, however, tested positive for this disease in 2001-2002 (Johnson and Averill-Murray 2003).

Jones tested the theory that prevalence of URTD would be highest near urban areas, as a result of disease transmission from released domestic tortoises (desert tortoises and exotic species). She tested four groups of tortoises along an urban gradient: captive tortoises; tortoises in high-visitor use areas, including the Mother's Day Fire area; tortoises in suburban areas, including the Rocking K Ranch-Saguaro National Park expansion area and Panther Peak area; and tortoises in remote areas. Jones examined each tortoise for clinical signs of URTD, collected blood to test for antibodies indicating previous exposure to the disease, and collected nasal lavage samples to determine if the tortoise was currently infected with the disease.

As expected, Jones found that the proportion of tortoises that tested positive for previous exposure to the disease differed along the urban gradient (Jones et al. 2005). However, the pattern was not exactly as predicted. A greater proportion of tortoises in suburban areas tested positive for previous exposure to the disease than all other areas, including captive tortoises. In fact, while a smaller proportion of tortoises in remote areas tested positive for previous exposure, the difference between remote and captive populations was remarkably small.

As part of the study, Jones evaluated whether disease status might affect tortoise home range sizes and seasonal activity patterns. She found that home range size did not differ between tortoises that had been previously exposed to URTD and tortoises that had not been exposed, and winter activity varied among individuals. While most tortoises remained in their winter hibernacula throughout the winter, three healthy females emerged from hibernation in February, consistent with spring activity patterns observed in other Sonoran and Mojave desert tortoises. Two male tortoises were also active during the winter, but unlike the females were exhibiting clinical signs of illness. This suggests that like other ectotherms, desert tortoises may use behavior to elevate body temperatures in response to infection. All original datasheets from this study were provided to the park, and a summary of results can be found in Jones et al. (2005).

Results from the Jones-Schwalbe study were also used as part of a larger study initiated by the Arizona Game and Fish Department, examining patterns of disease occurrence on a state-wide scale. For this larger study, Jones collected samples from captive and free-ranging tortoises throughout parks in the Phoenix area and protected land surrounding Kingman, Arizona. Jones found a higher prevalence of URTD in captive desert tortoises than those from high-visitor use areas in Phoenix and Kingman (Jones et al. 2006). When evaluating patterns on a state-wide scale, Jones found that a higher proportion of tortoises in the Tucson area had been previously exposed to URTD than that observed in the Phoenix or Kingman area. Detailed results of the Tucson and state-wide studies can be found in Jones's thesis (Jones 2008).

Zylstra-Steidl monitoring study, 2005-2006

Erin Zylstra, a graduate student of Robert Steidl at the University of Arizona and Saguaro National Park volunteer, conducted surveys for the desert tortoise in 2005-2006 in an attempt to compare the efficacy of different methods to be used as part of a long-term monitoring program. Monitoring species that are rare, cryptic, and have limited activity periods, like the desert tortoise, can be challenging. Current monitoring approaches use mark-recapture methods to estimate tortoise density on 1-km^2 or 1-mi^2 (0.39 m^2 or 2.6 km^2) plots, but are typically inefficient and limited in scope. Zylstra initiated the study to compare the efficiency and statistical power of distance-sampling and site-occupancy approaches as part of a long-term monitoring program for tortoises in the Sonoran Desert. Site-occupancy estimation is a relatively new approach for species with low rates of detection that uses repeated presence-absence surveys to estimate the proportion of area occupied.

In 2005, surveys were completed in the western portion of the Rincon Mountain District below 1150 m (3800 ft; Fig. 7), and in 2006, surveys were completed throughout the Tucson Mountain District (Fig. 8). To complete the distance-sampling portion of the project, 60 1-km (3281 ft) randomly-located transects were surveyed each year, and to complete the occupancy portion of the project, 20 3-ha (2.5 acre) randomly-located sites were each searched five times. Radio-transmitters were also attached to tortoises in the Rincon Mountain District (in the Mother's Day Fire area) and tortoises in the Tucson Mountain District (in the Panther Peak area and near the

Visitor Center) to estimate the proportion of animals available to be detected on distance-sampling surveys.

When combining results from the two districts, tortoise density was 31 adult tortoises/ha (12/mi^2; 95% CI = 21-44) and tortoise occupancy was 0.71 (95% CI = 0.59-0.83). Occupancy surveys were more efficient that distance-sampling surveys, and also had greater statistical power to detect annual declines in occupancy than distance sampling did to detect annual declines in density. These findings suggest that occupancy estimation may be a viable alternative to current desert tortoise monitoring strategies. All original data sheets from this study were provided to the park, and additional results from the study can be found in Zylstra et al. (2006) and Zylstra (2008b).

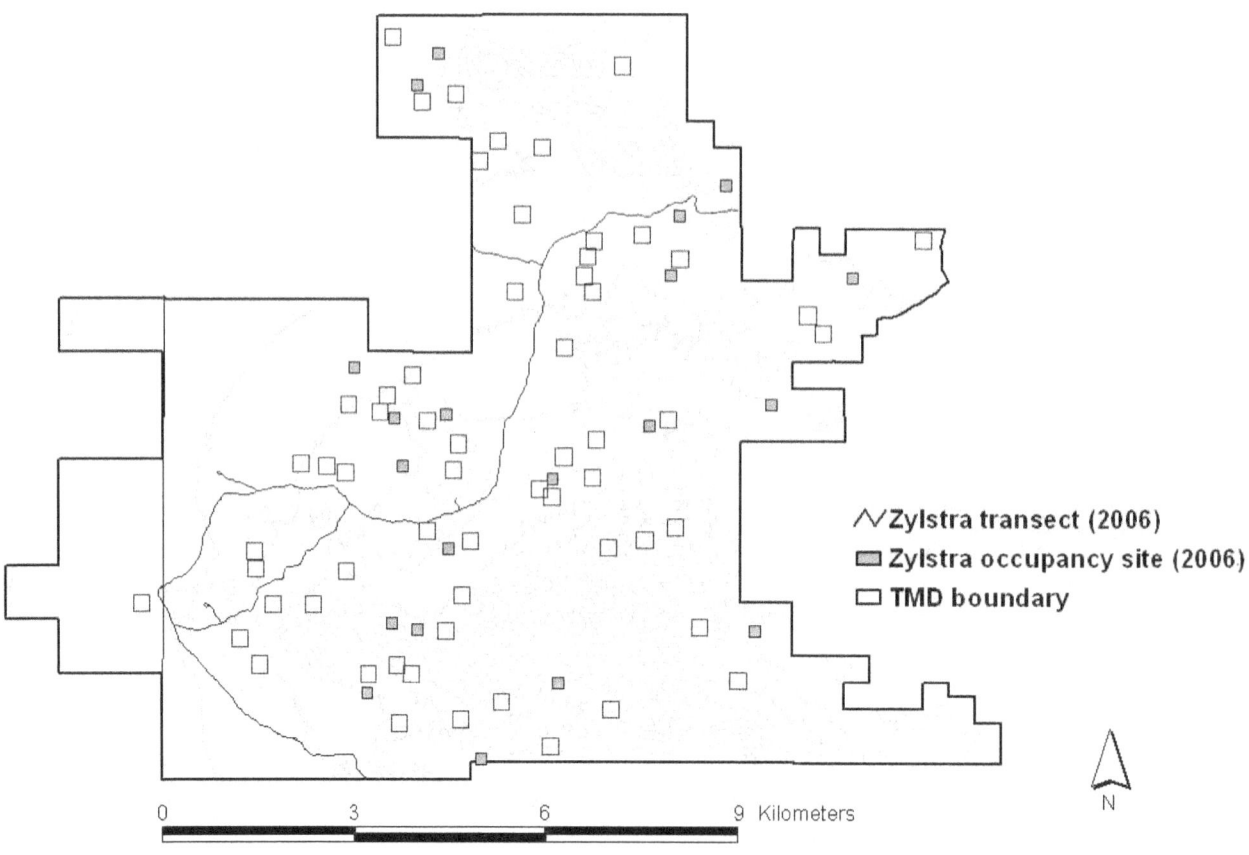

Figure 8. Distance-sampling transects and occupancy sites surveyed for desert tortoises in Saguaro National Park, Tucson Mountain District (TMD), 2006.

During the 2005-2006 surveys, Zylstra noted that an alarming number of tortoises in the Tucson Mountain District had injuries consistent with canine attacks. As a result, a study was undertaken to evaluate whether these injuries were likely caused by free-roaming dogs and whether injury rates varied over space or time. After conferring with veterinarians in the area, Zylstra determined that severe injuries to the gular and marginal scutes were likely caused by free-roaming dogs rather than mountain lions or coyotes. Mountain lion attacks on tortoises are typically fatal, and coyotes are not known to extensively chew the carapace, plastron, or gular horn of the tortoise. Further, injury rates were higher in the Tucson Mountain District than the Rincon Mountain District and have increased between 1996 and 2007. Given the high rate of development surrounding the Tucson Mountain District in recent years, it is likely that these injuries to tortoises were caused by released or abandoned pets. Zylstra (2008a) details results of this study evaluating the effects of free-roaming dogs on desert tortoise populations.

Desert tortoise research and education program, 2005-present

Park biologist Don Swann began working with high school and college interns on desert tortoise research projects in 1999, and found that students greatly benefitted from and enjoyed participating in these field-oriented projects. As a result, he began informally bringing small groups of students into the field to track radio-marked tortoises. In 2005, based on a small grant from the Friends of Saguaro National Park, Don and the park's interpretive division began formalizing this program, first in the Rincon Mountain District and then in the Tucson Mountain District. The Rincon Mountain District program was discontinued in 2006 after all the radios were removed from tortoises at the Mother's Day Fire site when the Cactus Forest Loop Road was closed for renovation.

Radio telemetry began in the Tucson Mountain District in July 2006 as part of the Zylstra-Steidl monitoring study. Telemetry was discontinued at Panther Peak in 2007, but was expanded in the Visitor Center area for the educational project. Small groups of high school students were taken into the field to track tortoises and collect data on weather, tortoise activity, movements, and habitat use. Daina Dajevskis and Chip Littlefield, Saguaro National Park employees at the Tucson Mountain District, worked on the desert tortoise education program, which was funded by the Friends and a Heritage grant from the Arizona Game and Fish Department. In 2007-2008, the program was expanded to include younger children (middle and elementary schools) who tracked tortoise shells, rather than live tortoises (Swann and Littlefield 2008a, b). In July 2008, radio-transmitters were removed from all but two of the tortoises that live in close proximity to the Visitor Center in the Tucson Mountain District.

Discussion

Since the mid-1980's, more than a dozen studies of desert tortoises have been conducted at Saguaro National Park. At least 12 agency reports, nine peer-reviewed scientific papers, four Master's theses, several book chapters, and countless talks at scientific conferences have resulted from this research. As a result of this work we have much a more complete picture of tortoise reproduction, diet, genetics, and diseases than we did 20 years ago, including a clear understanding of differences between tortoises in the Sonoran Desert and tortoises in the Mojave Desert.

Interpretive rangers at Saguaro National Park have in turn incorporated many of these research results into programs on desert tortoises for the public and school children. In addition to the education program described in this report, programs on the natural history and conservation of desert tortoises have been an important part of Junior Ranger camps, interpretive walks, and patio programs at the park. Resource managers and interpreters worked together to develop site bulletins, slide shows, travelling trunks, and other resources that are used in school and park programs focused on the unique biology of the Sonoran Desert tortoise. Each year, in cooperation with many of the organizations that support tortoise research, the park issues a press release related to tortoise conservation. This press release, which comes out during the tortoise activity season in August, provides information regarding basic natural history of the desert tortoise and what people can do to help protect tortoises. It has led to many newspaper articles and significant television coverage over the past several years.

Most studies on desert tortoises in Saguaro National Park have been sponsored or supported by the park, which has an important interest in protecting this charismatic species. The National Park Service has funded some of these studies, while other studies have received funding or have otherwise been supported by a great diversity of other organizations and agencies. These organizations include the Arizona Game and Fish Department, University of Arizona, U.S. Geological Survey, Smithsonian Institute, Western National Parks and Monuments Association, Friends of Saguaro National Park, Desert Southwest Cooperative Ecosystems Studies Unit, T&E Inc., Rincon Institute, and the Arizona-Sonora Desert Museum. Park neighbors, particularly the owners of the Rocking K Ranch, have allowed researchers to work on both sides of the boundary fence. The partnerships created between the National Park Service and other organizations have helped to place knowledge about this species within a larger geographic and ecological context, and have benefited tortoise management not only in Saguaro National Park, but throughout Arizona.

Often, data from research conducted in national parks are never recovered by the park, limiting the value of these data for use in long-term monitoring and future scientific studies. Most of the data from studies on tortoises at Saguaro National Park, however, are available because of the close collaboration of the many organizations involved. Within the park, information on the distribution and abundance of tortoises has been used in planning efforts, such as the placement of trails to avoid direct disruption of areas with high densities of desert tortoise shelter-sites, as well as in educational efforts to reduce the threats posed by domestic dogs. Identification of areas important for the desert tortoise in the park has also influenced the allocation of efforts expended to control non-native buffelgrass, which has become the highest resource management priority at the park.

Outside the park, results of tortoise research, particularly research on genetics, diet, reproduction, and monitoring techniques, have influenced long-term management efforts throughout Arizona. For example, research documenting the lack of genetic differentiation among tortoise populations in the Tucson area (Edwards et al. 2002, 2004a) indicates that augmentation of small or declining populations with additional individuals might be a viable option for preserving these populations in the future. Similarly, research on tortoise diet (Oftedal 2007) provides valuable information for managers of public lands with multiple uses that include protection of tortoises and livestock grazing.

Possibly the greatest benefit of research on a long-lived species like the desert tortoise is that it provides a long-term perspective which is often lacking in management of public lands.

Individual tortoises studied in the 1980's by Audrey Goldsmith continue to be observed in the park, in the same areas they occupied more than 20 years ago. Although we as humans must live very much in the day-to-day and face problems that must be addressed immediately, national parks are uniquely mandated to protect resources for visitors far into the future. Living in the wild for more than 50 years, and for perhaps as many as 100 years, desert tortoises offer a reminder that we would do well to devote at least a small amount of our energy to understanding longer-term processes, both human and ecological. It is our hope that future managers of Saguaro National Park and researchers will benefit from and build upon the results and resources provided by the studies described in this paper.

Literature Cited

Anderson, D. R., K. P. Burnham, B. C. Lubow, L. Thomas, P. S. Corn, P. A. Medica, and R. W. Marlow. 2001. Field trials of line transect methods applied to estimation of desert tortoise abundance. Journal of Wildlife Management **65**: 583-597.

Aslan, C. E., A. Schaeffer, and D. E. Swann. 2003. *Gopherus agassizii* (Desert Tortoise) elevational range. Herpetological Review **34**: 57.

Averill-Murray, R. C. 2002. Reproduction of *Gopherus agassizii* in the Sonoran Desert, Arizona. Chelonian Conservation and Biology **4**: 295-301.

Averill-Murray, R. C., and A. Averill-Murray. 2005. Regional-scale estimation of density and habitat use in the desert tortoise (*Gopherus agassizii*) in Arizona. Journal of Herpetology **39**: 65-72.

Averill-Murray, R. C. and D. E. Swann. 2002. Impacts of urbanization on desert tortoises at Saguaro National Park: tortoise density adjacent to the Rocking K Ranch development. Arizona Game and Fish Department Nongame and Endangered Wildlife Report 199. Phoenix, AZ.

Averill-Murray, R. C., A. P. Woodman, and J. M. Howland. 2002. Population ecology of the Sonoran desert tortoise in Arizona. Pages 109-134 *in* T. R. Van Devender, editor. The Sonoran desert tortoise: natural history, biology, and conservation. University of Arizona Press, Tucson, AZ.

Barrett, S. L. 1990. Home range and habitat of the desert tortoise (*Xerobates agasszii*) in the Picacho Mountains of Arizona. Herpetologica **46**: 202-206.

Edwards, T. 2003. Desert tortoise conservation genetics. M.S. Thesis, University of Arizona, Tucson.

Edwards, T., C. S. Goldberg, M. G. Kaplan, C. R. Schwalbe, and D. E. Swann. 2003. PCR primers for microsatellite loci in desert tortoise *(Gopherus agassizii*, Testudinidae)*. Molecular Ecology Notes **3**: 589-591.

Edwards, T., C. R. Schwable, D.E. Swann, and C.S. Goldberg. 2002. Desert tortoise conservation genetics: genetic variability among and within Sonoran populations. Final report, Arizona Game and Fish Department Heritage Fund IIPAM Project I20012. Phoenix, AZ.

Edwards, T., C. R. Schwalbe, D. E. Swann, and C. S. Goldberg. 2004a. Implications of anthropogenic landscape change on inter-population movements of the desert tortoise (*Gopherus agassizii*). Conservation Genetics **5**: 485-499.

Edwards, T., E. W. Stitt, C. R. Schwalbe, and D. E. Swann. 2004b. Desert Tortoise (*Gopherus agassizii*): Movement. Herpetological Review **35**: 381-382.

Esque, T. C., A. Búrquez M., C. R. Schwalbe, T. R. Van Devender, P. J. Anning, and M. J. Nijhuis. 2002. Fire ecology of the Sonoran desert tortoise. Pages 312-333 *in* T. R. Van Devender, editor. The Sonoran desert tortoise: natural history, biology, and conservation. University of Arizona Press, Tucson, AZ.

Esque, T.C., C.R. Schwalbe, L.A. DeFalco, R.B. Duncan, and T.J. Hughes. 2003. Effects of desert wildfires on desert tortoise (*Gopherus agassizii*) and other small vertebrates. Southwestern Naturalist **48**: 103-111.

Esque, T.C., C.R. Schwalbe, and R.B. Duncan. 1994. Survey for the effects of fire on saguaros and desert tortoises at Saguaro National Monument. Proposal to Saguaro National Monument. Tucson, AZ.

Esque, T. C., C. R. Schwalbe, D. F. Haines, and W. L. Halvorson. 2004. Saguaros under siege: invasive species and fire. Desert Plants **20**: 49-55.

Germano, D. J., R. B. Bury, T. C. Esque, T. H. Fritts, and P. A. Medica. 1994. Range and habitats of the desert tortoise. Pages 73-84 *in* R. B. Bury and D. J. Germano, editors. Biology of North American tortoises. National Biological Survey, Fish and Wildlife Research 13, Washington, D.C.

Goldsmith, A., and W. W. Shaw. 1990. Report on desert tortoise telemetry studies in Saguaro National Monument, 1989. Final Report to Southwest Parks and Monuments Association. Tucson, AZ.

Jacobson, E. R., J. M Gaskin, M. B. Brown, R. K. Harris, C. H. Gardiner, J. L. LaPointe, H. P. Adams, and C. Reggiardo. 1991. Chronic upper respiratory tract disease of free-ranging desert tortoises, *Xerobates agassizii*. Journal of Wildlife Diseases **27**: 296-316.

Johnson, J. D., and R. C. Averill-Murray. 2004. 2002 health surveys of Sonoran desert tortoises. Page 20 *in* Duncan, D. K., G. Stewart, M. Tuegel, T. B. Egan, and D. Pond, editors. Proceedings of the 2002 and 2003 Symposia of the Desert Tortoise Council, Wrightwood, CA. Ominipress, Madison, WI.

Jones, C. A. 2008. *Mycoplasma agassizii* in the Sonoran population of the desert tortoise in Arizona. M.S. Thesis, University of Arizona, Tucson.

Jones, C.A., C.R. Schwalbe, D.E. Swann, D.B. Prival, and W.W. Shaw. 2005. *Mycoplasma agassizii* in Desert Tortoises. Final report to Arizona Game and Fish Department Heritage Fund Project U03005. Phoenix, AZ.

Jones, C. A., C. R. Schwalbe, and W. W. Shaw. 2006. Health status of urban desert tortoises. Final Report to the Arizona Game and Fish Department. Phoenix, AZ.

Knowles, C. 1989. A survey for diseased desert tortoises in and near the Desert Tortoise Natural Area. Report to the Bureau of Land Management, contract no. CA 950-(T9-23). Riverside, CA.

Murphy, R. W., K. H. Berry, T. Edwards, and A. M. McLuckie. 2007. A genetic assessment of the recovery units for the Mojave population of the desert tortoise, *Gopherus agassizii*. Chelonian Conservation and Biology **6**: 229-251.

Murray, R. C. 1995. Amphibian and reptile inventory. Pages 50-78 *in* L. K. Harris and C.R. Schwalbe, editors. Wildlife inventory of the Rincon Valley. Final report to Arizona Game and Fish Department Heritage Fund Project U93007. Phoenix, AZ.

Murray, R. C. 1996. Amphibian and reptile inventory. Pages 31-46 *in* L. K. Harris, editor. Wildlife inventory of the Saguaro National Park expansion area. Final Report to Saguaro National Park, Tucson, AZ.

Oftedal, O. T. 2007. Nutritional ecology of the Sonoran desert tortoise. Final report to the Arizona Game and Fish Department Heritage Fund Project I04004, Phoenix, AZ.

Riedle, J. D., and R. C. Averill-Murray. 2003. Disease incidence on Sonoran Desert long term monitoring plots. Pages 141-146 *in* Proceedings of the 2002 and 2003 Desert Tortoise Council Symposia.

Schwalbe, C. R., T. Edwards, E.W. Stitt, R. Averill-Murray, and D. E. Swann. 2002. Desert tortoises in a changing landscape: a long-term study at Saguaro National Park. Final report to Western National Parks Association and Saguaro National Park. Tucson, AZ.

Shaw, W. W., and A. Goldsmith. 1988. Final report on desert tortoise ecology, 1988. Final report to the Southwest Parks and Monuments Association. Tucson, AZ.

Shaw, W. W., A. Goldsmith, P. R. Krausman, and R. W. Mannan. 1987. Relationships between adjacent land uses and the wildlife resources of Saguaro National Monument. Research proposal prepared for Saguaro National Monument. Tucson, AZ.

Stebbins, R. C. 2003. A field guide to western reptiles and amphibians. Third edition. Houghton Mifflin, New York, NY.

Stitt, E. W. 2004. Demography, reproduction, and movements of desert tortoises (*Gopherus agassizii*) in the Rincon Mountains, Arizona. M.S. Thesis, University of Arizona, Tucson.

Stitt, E. W., and C. Davis. 2003. *Gopherus agassizii* (Desert Tortoise). Caliche mining. Herpetological Review **34**: 57.

Stitt, E. W., J. Cain, C. R. Schwalbe, and D. E. Swann. 2003a. Using infrared cameras to monitor burrow associates of desert tortoises at Saguaro National Park. Report to Western National Parks Association and Saguaro National Park. Tucson, AZ.

Stitt, E. W., C. R. Schwalbe, and D. E. Swann. 2003b. Signs of Gila monster predation on desert tortoise nests. Sonoran Herpetologist **16**: 113.

Stitt, E. W., C. R. Schwalbe, and D. E. Swann. 2005. Desert Tortoise (*Gopherus agassizii*). Association with Africanized bees. Herpetological Review **35**: 381.

Stitt, E.W., C. R. Schwalbe, D. E. Swann, R. C. Averill-Murray, and A.K. Blythe. 2003c. Sonoran Desert tortoise ecology and management: effects of land use change and urbanization on desert tortoises. Final report to Saguaro National Park. Tucson, AZ.

Swann, D.E., C. R. Schwalbe, T. Volz, and D. Prival. 2001. Effect of urban development on desert tortoises: summary of 2000 field season. Report to T&E, Inc. Cortaro, AZ.

Swann, D. E., R. C. Averill-Murray, and C. R. Schwalbe. 2002. Distance sampling for Sonoran desert tortoises. Journal of Wildlife Management **66**: 943-949.

Swann, D. E. and C. Littlefield. 2008a. Desert tortoise education program. Final report to Friends of Saguaro National Park, Earth Friends Wildlife Foundation, and Beth Spiva Timmons Foundation. Tucson, AZ.

Swann, D. E. and C. Littlefield. 2008b. Desert tortoise education program. Final report to Arizona Game and Fish Department Heritage Fund Project U08008, Phoenix, AZ.

U.S. Fish and Wildlife Service. 2004. Desert tortoise (Mojave population) recovery plan. U.S. Fish and Wildlife Service, Portland, OR.

U.S. Fish and Wildlife Service. 2006. Range-wide monitoring of the Mojave populations of the desert tortoise: 2001-2005 summary report. Desert Tortoise Recovery Office, U.S. Fish and Wildlife Service, Reno, NV.

Van Devender, T. R., and H. E. Lawler. 1995. Diet and nutrition of the desert tortoise (*Xerobates agassizi*) in the northeastern Sonoran Desert. Final Report to Saguaro National Park. Tucson, AZ.

Van Devender, T. R. 2002. The Sonoran desert tortoise: natural history, biology, and conservation. University of Arizona Press, Tucson.

Vaughn, S. 1984. Home range and habitat use of the desert tortoise in the Picacho Mountains, Pinal County, Arizona. M. S. Thesis. Arizona State University, Tempe.

Wirt, B. E, and R. H. Robichaux. 2001. Survey and monitoring of the desert tortoise, *Gopherus agassizii*, at Saguaro National Park. Final Report to Saguaro National Park. Tucson, AZ.

Zylstra, E. R. 2008a. Effects of free-roaming dogs on desert tortoise populations in Saguaro National Park. Final report to Saguaro National Park. Tucson, AZ.

Zylstra, E. R. 2008b. Evaluating monitoring strategies and habitat for tortoises in the Sonoran Desert. M.S. Thesis, University of Arizona, Tucson.

Zylstra, E. R., R. J. Steidl, and D. E. Swann. 2006. Monitoring strategies for the Sonoran desert tortoise. Final report to the Arizona Game and Fish Department. Phoenix, AZ.

Appendix A. Name or numbers and locations of visual encounter transects, distance-sampling transects, mark-recapture plots, and occupancy sites surveyed for desert tortoises in Saguaro National Park, Tucson, Arizona, USA, 1988-2006.

Transect/Plot ID	Type[a]	Project[b]	District[c]	General location	UTMs[d]	Easting[e]	Northing[e]	Corner[f]	Source of location info.[g]
F1E	VET	A	RMD	Mica View Picnic	Unavailable	--	--	--	Wirt maps
F2E	VET	A	RMD	End of Speedway	Unavailable	--	--	--	Wirt maps
F3E	VET	A	RMD	Loma Verde Wash	Unavailable	--	--	--	Wirt maps
F4E	VET	A	RMD	Javelina Picnic Area	Unavailable	--	--	--	Wirt maps
F5E	VET	A	RMD	Broadway Rd.	Unavailable	--	--	--	Wirt maps
S1E	VET	A	RMD	Base of Rincons	Unavailable	--	--	--	Wirt maps
S2E	VET	A	RMD	Base of Rincons	Unavailable	--	--	--	Wirt maps
S3E	VET	A	RMD	Lower Box Canyon	Unavailable	--	--	--	Wirt maps
S4E	VET	A	RMD	Cactus Forest Trail	Unavailable	--	--	--	Wirt maps
S5E	VET	A	RMD	Lower Box Canyon	Unavailable	--	--	--	Wirt maps
S6E	VET	A	RMD	Douglas Spring Trail	Unavailable	--	--	--	Wirt maps
S7E	VET	A	RMD	Madrona Ranger Station	Unavailable	--	--	--	Wirt maps
S8E	VET	A	RMD	Madrona Canyon	Unavailable	--	--	--	Wirt maps
S9E	VET	A	RMD	Rocking K Ranch	Unavailable	--	--	--	Wirt maps
F1W	VET	A	TMD	Kinney and Sandario	Unavailable	--	--	--	Wirt maps
F2W	VET	A	TMD	Kinney and Hohokam	Unavailable	--	--	--	Wirt maps
F3W	VET	A	TMD	N of Ez-Kim-In-Zin	Unavailable	--	--	--	Wirt maps
F4W	VET	A	TMD	Signal Hill	Unavailable	--	--	--	Wirt maps
F5W	VET	A	TMD	GoldenGate/PictureRocks	Unavailable	--	--	--	Wirt maps
F6W	VET	A	TMD	GoldenGate/PictureRocks	Unavailable	--	--	--	Wirt maps
S1W	VET	A	TMD	Sus Picnic Area	Unavailable	--	--	--	Wirt maps
S2W	VET	A	TMD	Wasson Peak Trailhead	Unavailable	--	--	--	Wirt maps
S3W	VET	A	TMD	Hohokam to Hugh Norris	Unavailable	--	--	--	Wirt maps
S4W	VET	A	TMD	Kings Canyon	Unavailable	--	--	--	Wirt maps
S5W	VET	A	TMD	Red Hills	Unavailable	--	--	--	Wirt maps
S6W	VET	A	TMD	Pima Farm Rd	Unavailable	--	--	--	Wirt maps
S7W	VET	A	TMD	Picture Rocks Canyon	Unavailable	--	--	--	Wirt maps
S8W	VET	A	TMD	NW Contzen Pass	Unavailable	--	--	--	Wirt maps

Transect/Plot ID	Type[a]	Project[b]	District[c]	General location	UTMs[d]	Easting[e]	Northing[e]	Corner[f]	Source of location info.[g]
S9W	VET	A	TMD	Contzen Pass	Unavailable	--	--	--	Wirt maps
S10W	VET	A	TMD	Camino del Cerro	Unavailable	--	--	--	Wirt maps
S11W	VET	A	TMD	Camino del Cerro	Unavailable	--	--	--	Wirt maps
S12W	VET	A	TMD	Red Hills Visitor Center	Unavailable	--	--	--	Wirt maps
Javelina	MR	A, B	RMD	Javelina Picnic Area	Approx.	525210	3557745	SW	Wirt and Robichaux 2001
Javelina	MR	A, B	RMD	Javelina Picnic Area	Approx.	525210	3558745	NW	Wirt and Robichaux 2001
Javelina	MR	A, B	RMD	Javelina Picnic Area	Approx.	526210	3558745	NE	Wirt and Robichaux 2001
Javelina	MR	A, B	RMD	Javelina Picnic Area	Approx.	526210	3557745	SE	Wirt and Robichaux 2001
Goldsmith plot	MR	A	RMD	SNP Expansion Area	Approx.	527202	3556862	SW	Misc. project materials
Goldsmith plot	MR	A	RMD	SNP Expansion Area	Approx.	527202	3557550	NW	Misc. project materials
Goldsmith plot	MR	A	RMD	SNP Expansion Area	Approx.	530421	3557550	NE	Misc. project materials
Goldsmith plot	MR	A	RMD	SNP Expansion Area	Approx.	530421	3556862	SE	Misc. project materials
1	VET	B	RMD	Chimenea Canyon	Unavailable	--	--	--	Wirt maps
2	VET	B	RMD	Cactus Forest Trail	Unavailable	--	--	--	Wirt maps
3	VET	B	RMD	Loma Verde Wash	Unavailable	--	--	--	Wirt maps
4	VET	B	RMD	End of Speedway	Unavailable	--	--	--	Wirt maps
5	VET	B	RMD	Cactus Forest Trail	Unavailable	--	--	--	Wirt maps
6	VET	B	RMD	Speedway and Broadway	Unavailable	--	--	--	Wirt maps
7	VET	B	RMD	Douglas Spring Trail	Unavailable	--	--	--	Wirt maps
8	VET	B	RMD	Base of Rincons	Unavailable	--	--	--	Wirt maps
9	VET	B	RMD	Madrona Ranger Station	Unavailable	--	--	--	Wirt maps
10	VET	B	RMD	Base of Rincons	Unavailable	--	--	--	Wirt maps
11	VET	B	RMD	Chimenea Canyon	Unavailable	--	--	--	Wirt maps
12	VET	B	RMD	Tanque Verde Trail	Unavailable	--	--	--	Wirt maps
13	VET	B	RMD	Upper Rincon Creek	Unavailable	--	--	--	Wirt maps
1	VET	B	TMD	Panther Peak	Unavailable	--	--	--	Wirt maps
2	VET	B	TMD	Panther Peak	Unavailable	--	--	--	Wirt maps
3	VET	B	TMD	Signal Hill	Unavailable	--	--	--	Wirt maps
4	VET	B	TMD	W of Red Hills	Unavailable	--	--	--	Wirt maps
5	VET	B	TMD	N of Ez-Kim-In-Zin	Unavailable	--	--	--	Wirt maps
6	VET	B	TMD	NW of Contzen Pass	Unavailable	--	--	--	Wirt maps
7	VET	B	TMD	Ez-Kim-In-Zin Hills	Unavailable	--	--	--	Wirt maps
8	VET	B	TMD	Picture Rocks Canyon	Unavailable	--	--	--	Wirt maps
9	VET	B	TMD	GoldenGate/PictureRocks	Unavailable	--	--	--	Wirt maps
10	VET	B	TMD	Camino del Cerro	Unavailable	--	--	--	Wirt maps

Transect/Plot ID	Type[a]	Project[b]	District[c]	General location	UTMs[d]	Easting[e]	Northing[e]	Corner[f]	Source of location info.[g]
10B	VET	B	TMD	Camino del Cerro	Unavailable	--	--	--	Wirt maps
11	VET	B	TMD	Yuma Mine	Unavailable	--	--	--	Wirt maps
12	VET	B	TMD	End of Sweetwater Rd	Unavailable	--	--	--	Wirt maps
13	VET	B	TMD	End of Abington Rd	Unavailable	--	--	--	Wirt maps
14	VET	B	TMD	Radio Tower Ridge	Unavailable	--	--	--	Wirt maps
15	VET	B	TMD	Wasson Peak	Unavailable	--	--	--	Wirt maps
16	VET	B	TMD	Safford Peak	Unavailable	--	--	--	Wirt maps
17	VET	B	TMD	Amole Peak	Unavailable	--	--	--	Wirt maps
Mother's Day Fire	MR	B	RMD	Mother's Day Fire	Approx.	527825	3561390	SW	Wirt and Robichaux 2001
Mother's Day Fire	MR	B	RMD	Mother's Day Fire	Approx.	527825	3562390	NW	Wirt and Robichaux 2001
Mother's Day Fire	MR	B	RMD	Mother's Day Fire	Approx.	528825	3562390	NE	Wirt and Robichaux 2001
Mother's Day Fire	MR	B	RMD	Mother's Day Fire	Approx.	528825	3561390	SE	Wirt and Robichaux 2001
Panther Peak	MR	B	TMD	S of Panther Peak	Approx.	484440	3577180	SW	Wirt and Robichaux 2001
Panther Peak	MR	B	TMD	S of Panther Peak	Approx.	484440	3578180	NW	Wirt and Robichaux 2001
Panther Peak	MR	B	TMD	S of Panther Peak	Approx.	485440	3578180	NE	Wirt and Robichaux 2001
Panther Peak	MR	B	TMD	S of Panther Peak	Approx.	485440	3577180	SE	Wirt and Robichaux 2001
1A	DS	C	RMD	Rocking K Ranch	Provided	527171	3556506	SW	SNP server
1B	DS	C	RMD	Rocking K Ranch	Provided	527171	3556156	SW	SNP server
1C	DS	C	RMD	Rocking K Ranch	Provided	527171	3555806	SW	SNP server
1D	DS	C	RMD	Rocking K Ranch	Provided	527171	3555456	SW	SNP server
2A	DS	C	RMD	Rocking K Ranch	Provided	527521	3556506	SW	SNP server
2B	DS	C	RMD	Rocking K Ranch	Provided	527521	3556156	SW	SNP server
2C	DS	C	RMD	Rocking K Ranch	Provided	527521	3555806	SW	SNP server
2D	DS	C	RMD	Rocking K Ranch	Provided	527521	3555456	SW	SNP server
2E	DS	C	RMD	Rocking K Ranch	Provided	527521	3555106	SW	SNP server
3A	DS	C	RMD	Rocking K Ranch	Provided	527871	3556506	SW	SNP server
3B	DS	C	RMD	Rocking K Ranch	Provided	527871	3556156	SW	SNP server
3C	DS	C	RMD	Rocking K Ranch	Provided	527871	3555806	SW	SNP server
3D	DS	C	RMD	Rocking K Ranch	Provided	527871	3555456	SW	SNP server
3E	DS	C	RMD	Rocking K Ranch	Provided	527871	3555106	SW	SNP server
4A	DS	C	RMD	Rocking K Ranch	Provided	528221	3556506	SW	SNP server
4B	DS	C	RMD	Rocking K Ranch	Provided	528221	3556156	SW	SNP server
4C	DS	C	RMD	Rocking K Ranch	Provided	528221	3555806	SW	SNP server
4D	DS	C	RMD	Rocking K Ranch	Provided	528221	3555456	SW	SNP server
4E	DS	C	RMD	Rocking K Ranch	Provided	528221	3555106	SW	SNP server

Transect/Plot ID	Type[a]	Project[b]	District[c]	General location	UTMs[d]	Easting[e]	Northing[e]	Corner[f]	Source of location info.[g]
4F	DS	C	RMD	Rocking K Ranch	Provided	528221	3554756	SW	SNP server
5A	DS	C	RMD	Rocking K Ranch	Provided	528571	3556506	SW	SNP server
5B	DS	C	RMD	Rocking K Ranch	Provided	528571	3556156	SW	SNP server
5C	DS	C	RMD	Rocking K Ranch	Provided	528571	3555806	SW	SNP server
5D	DS	C	RMD	Rocking K Ranch	Provided	528571	3555456	SW	SNP server
5E	DS	C	RMD	Rocking K Ranch	Provided	528571	3555106	SW	SNP server
5F	DS	C	RMD	Rocking K Ranch	Provided	528571	3554756	SW	SNP server
5G	DS	C	RMD	Rocking K Ranch	Provided	528571	3554406	SW	SNP server
5H	DS	C	RMD	Rocking K Ranch	Provided	528571	3554056	SW	SNP server
6A	DS	C	RMD	Rocking K Ranch	Provided	528921	3556506	SW	SNP server
6B	DS	C	RMD	Rocking K Ranch	Provided	528921	3556156	SW	SNP server
6C	DS	C	RMD	Rocking K Ranch	Provided	528921	3555806	SW	SNP server
6D	DS	C	RMD	Rocking K Ranch	Provided	528921	3555456	SW	SNP server
6E	DS	C	RMD	Rocking K Ranch	Provided	528921	3555106	SW	SNP server
6F	DS	C	RMD	Rocking K Ranch	Provided	528921	3554756	SW	SNP server
8A	DS	C	RMD	SNP Expansion Area	Provided	529622	3556506	SW	SNP server
8B	DS	C	RMD	SNP Expansion Area	Provided	529622	3556156	SW	SNP server
8C	DS	C	RMD	SNP Expansion Area	Provided	529622	3555806	SW	SNP server
8D	DS	C	RMD	SNP Expansion Area	Provided	529622	3555456	SW	SNP server
8E	DS	C	RMD	SNP Expansion Area	Provided	529622	3555106	SW	SNP server
8F	DS	C	RMD	SNP Expansion Area	Provided	529622	3554756	SW	SNP server
8G	DS	C	RMD	SNP Expansion Area	Provided	529622	3554406	SW	SNP server
9A	DS	C	RMD	SNP Expansion Area	Provided	529972	3556506	SW	SNP server
9B	DS	C	RMD	SNP Expansion Area	Provided	529972	3556156	SW	SNP server
9C	DS	C	RMD	SNP Expansion Area	Provided	529972	3555806	SW	SNP server
9D	DS	C	RMD	SNP Expansion Area	Provided	529972	3555456	SW	SNP server
10A	DS	C	RMD	SNP Expansion Area	Provided	530322	3556506	SW	SNP server
10B	DS	C	RMD	SNP Expansion Area	Provided	530322	3556156	SW	SNP server
10C	DS	C	RMD	SNP Expansion Area	Provided	530322	3555806	SW	SNP server
10E	DS	C	RMD	SNP Expansion Area	Provided	530322	3555106	SW	SNP server
10F	DS	C	RMD	SNP Expansion Area	Provided	530322	3554756	SW	SNP server
10G	DS	C	RMD	SNP Expansion Area	Provided	530322	3554406	SW	SNP server
11A	DS	C	RMD	SNP Expansion Area	Provided	530672	3556506	SW	SNP server
11B	DS	C	RMD	SNP Expansion Area	Provided	530672	3556156	SW	SNP server
11C	DS	C	RMD	SNP Expansion Area	Provided	530672	3555806	SW	SNP server

Transect/Plot ID	Type[a]	Project[b]	District[c]	General location	UTMs[d]	Easting[e]	Northing[e]	Corner[f]	Source of location info.[g]
11D	DS	C	RMD	SNP Expansion Area	Provided	530672	3555456	SW	SNP server
12A	DS	C	RMD	SNP Expansion Area	Provided	531022	3556506	SW	SNP server
12D	DS	C	RMD	SNP Expansion Area	Provided	531022	3555456	SW	SNP server
13A	DS	C	RMD	SNP Expansion Area	Provided	531372	3556506	SW	SNP server
13B	DS	C	RMD	SNP Expansion Area	Provided	531372	3556156	SW	SNP server
13C	DS	C	RMD	SNP Expansion Area	Provided	531372	3555806	SW	SNP server
13D	DS	C	RMD	SNP Expansion Area	Provided	531372	3555456	SW	SNP server
14A	DS	C	RMD	SNP Expansion Area	Provided	531722	3556506	SW	SNP server
14B	DS	C	RMD	SNP Expansion Area	Provided	531722	3556156	SW	SNP server
14C	DS	C	RMD	SNP Expansion Area	Provided	531722	3555806	SW	SNP server
15A	DS	C	RMD	SNP Expansion Area	Provided	532072	3556506	SW	SNP server
15B	DS	C	RMD	SNP Expansion Area	Provided	532072	3556156	SW	SNP server
15C	DS	C	RMD	SNP Expansion Area	Provided	532072	3555806	SW	SNP server
15D	DS	C	RMD	SNP Expansion Area	Provided	532072	3555456	SW	SNP server
T107	DS	D	RMD	Lower Wildhorse Canyon	Provided	528473	3564686	SW	Zylstra et al. 2006
T109	DS	D	RMD	Javelina Rocks	Provided	526476	3559326	SW	Zylstra et al. 2006
T111	DS	D	RMD	Mother's Day Fire Area	Provided	528044	3561266	SW	Zylstra et al. 2006
T113	DS	D	RMD	Wentworth Trail	Provided	527926	3565057	SW	Zylstra et al. 2006
T117	DS	D	RMD	Javelina Picnic Area	Provided	525954	3557686	SW	Zylstra et al. 2006
T119	DS	D	RMD	Douglas Spring Trail	Provided	532101	3565811	SW	Zylstra et al. 2006
T120	DS	D	RMD	Base of Rincons	Provided	529805	3564473	SW	Zylstra et al. 2006
T121	DS	D	RMD	Javelina Picnic Area	Provided	525770	3557505	SW	Zylstra et al. 2006
T123	DS	D	RMD	Upper Wildhorse Canyon	Provided	529493	3563361	SW	Zylstra et al. 2006
T124	DS	D	RMD	Cactus Forest Loop	Provided	527139	3562139	SW	Zylstra et al. 2006
T128	DS	D	RMD	Douglas Spring Trail	Provided	530950	3565796	SW	Zylstra et al. 2006
T130	DS	D	RMD	Shantz Trail	Provided	528958	3566231	SW	Zylstra et al. 2006
T134	DS	D	RMD	Cactus Forest Loop	Provided	526875	3561088	SW	Zylstra et al. 2006
T136	DS	D	RMD	Cactus Forest Loop	Provided	527526	3562898	SW	Zylstra et al. 2006
T142	DS	D	RMD	Wildhorse Trail	Provided	529628	3565496	SW	Zylstra et al. 2006
T152	DS	D	RMD	Wildhorse Trail	Provided	529540	3565223	SW	Zylstra et al. 2006
T153	DS	D	RMD	Wentworth Trail	Provided	527534	3565310	SW	Zylstra et al. 2006
T154	DS	D	RMD	Lower Loma Verde Wash	Provided	528041	3562661	SW	Zylstra et al. 2006
T155	DS	D	RMD	Upper Wildhorse Canyon	Provided	529638	3563961	SW	Zylstra et al. 2006
T156	DS	D	RMD	Cactus Forest Loop	Provided	526825	3561532	SW	Zylstra et al. 2006
T157	DS	D	RMD	Base of Rincons	Provided	530173	3564588	SW	Zylstra et al. 2006

Transect/Plot ID	Type[a]	Project[b]	District[c]	General location	UTMs[d]	Easting[e]	Northing[e]	Corner[f]	Source of location info.[g]
T158	DS	D	RMD	Cactus Forest Loop	Provided	525146	3559557	SW	Zylstra et al. 2006
T160	DS	D	RMD	Freeman Rd	Provided	524876	3563608	SW	Zylstra et al. 2006
T161	DS	D	RMD	Upper Wildhorse Canyon	Provided	529732	3563144	SW	Zylstra et al. 2006
T162	DS	D	RMD	Douglas Spring Trail	Provided	530727	3565423	SW	Zylstra et al. 2006
T163	DS	D	RMD	Base of Rincons	Provided	530233	3564113	SW	Zylstra et al. 2006
T165	DS	D	RMD	Wentworth Trail	Provided	526786	3565566	SW	Zylstra et al. 2006
T166	DS	D	RMD	Wentworth Trail	Provided	528240	3565460	SW	Zylstra et al. 2006
T167	DS	D	RMD	Mother's Day Fire Area	Provided	527638	3561568	SW	Zylstra et al. 2006
T168	DS	D	RMD	Cactus Forest Loop	Provided	525506	3560632	SW	Zylstra et al. 2006
T170	DS	D	RMD	Cactus Forest Loop	Provided	525615	3561745	SW	Zylstra et al. 2006
T172	DS	D	RMD	Wentworth Trail	Provided	528296	3565038	SW	Zylstra et al. 2006
T173	DS	D	RMD	Loma Verde Trail	Provided	527260	3563538	SW	Zylstra et al. 2006
T174	DS	D	RMD	Wentworth Trail	Provided	528608	3564973	SW	Zylstra et al. 2006
T179	DS	D	RMD	Base of Rincons	Provided	530298	3565057	SW	Zylstra et al. 2006
T180	DS	D	RMD	Freeman and Broadway	Provided	525195	3564406	SW	Zylstra et al. 2006
T182	DS	D	RMD	Squeeze Pen Trail	Provided	528206	3564156	SW	Zylstra et al. 2006
T183	DS	D	RMD	Mother's Day Fire Area	Provided	528418	3561653	SW	Zylstra et al. 2006
T188	DS	D	RMD	Upper Wildhorse Canyon	Provided	529396	3563585	SW	Zylstra et al. 2006
T189	DS	D	RMD	Squeeze Pen Trail	Provided	528082	3563223	SW	Zylstra et al. 2006
T190	DS	D	RMD	Cactus Forest Loop	Provided	526760	3559825	SW	Zylstra et al. 2006
T191	DS	D	RMD	Upper Wildhorse Canyon	Provided	529753	3562961	SW	Zylstra et al. 2006
T193	DS	D	RMD	Wentworth Trail	Provided	530043	3565542	SW	Zylstra et al. 2006
T198	DS	D	RMD	Cactus Forest Trail	Provided	526101	3560456	SW	Zylstra et al. 2006
T202	DS	D	RMD	Javelina Picnic Area	Provided	525384	3557561	SW	Zylstra et al. 2006
T211	DS	D	RMD	Douglas Spring Trail	Provided	531807	3565742	SW	Zylstra et al. 2006
T213	DS	D	RMD	Douglas Spring Trail	Provided	529759	3566079	SW	Zylstra et al. 2006
T214	DS	D	RMD	Cactus Forest Loop	Provided	526974	3559590	SW	Zylstra et al. 2006
T215	DS	D	RMD	Loma Verde Trail	Provided	527487	3563495	SW	Zylstra et al. 2006
T216	DS	D	RMD	Cactus Forest Trail	Provided	525866	3559450	SW	Zylstra et al. 2006
T218	DS	D	RMD	Mica View Picnic Area	Provided	525971	3563903	SW	Zylstra et al. 2006
T221	DS	D	RMD	Douglas Spring Trail	Provided	531730	3565404	SW	Zylstra et al. 2006
T222	DS	D	RMD	Base of Rincons	Provided	529908	3564263	SW	Zylstra et al. 2006
T224	DS	D	RMD	Douglas Spring Trail	Provided	532480	3566278	SW	Zylstra et al. 2006
T231	DS	D	RMD	Base of Rincons	Provided	530424	3564418	SW	Zylstra et al. 2006
T237	DS	D	RMD	Squeeze Pen Trail	Provided	528434	3563534	SW	Zylstra et al. 2006

Transect/Plot ID	Type[a]	Project[b]	District[c]	General location	UTMs[d]	Easting[e]	Northing[e]	Corner[f]	Source of location info.[g]
T238	DS	D	RMD	Mother's Day Fire Area	Provided	527798	3562394	SW	Zylstra et al. 2006
T240	DS	D	RMD	Javelina Picnic Area	Provided	525640	3558213	SW	Zylstra et al. 2006
T247	DS	D	RMD	Javelina Picnic Area	Provided	525501	3557905	SW	Zylstra et al. 2006
T262	DS	D	RMD	Javelina Picnic Area	Provided	525217	3557174	SW	Zylstra et al. 2006
P01	OCC	D	RMD	Douglas Spring Trail	Provided	531019	3566350	SW	Zylstra et al. 2006
P03	OCC	D	RMD	Garwood Trail	Provided	529761	3565475	SW	Zylstra et al. 2006
P04	OCC	D	RMD	Mother's Day Fire Area	Provided	528508	3562412	SW	Zylstra et al. 2006
P12	OCC	D	RMD	Cactus Forest Loop	Provided	527060	3562622	SW	Zylstra et al. 2006
P17	OCC	D	RMD	Freeman Rd	Provided	524759	3562010	SW	Zylstra et al. 2006
P18	OCC	D	RMD	Squeeze Pen Trail	Provided	528035	3563859	SW	Zylstra et al. 2006
P19	OCC	D	RMD	Upper Wildhorse Canyon	Provided	530001	3563369	SW	Zylstra et al. 2006
P21	OCC	D	RMD	Wentworth Trail	Provided	528233	3565698	SW	Zylstra et al. 2006
P22	OCC	D	RMD	Carrillo Trail	Provided	529021	3564583	SW	Zylstra et al. 2006
P24	OCC	D	RMD	Tanque Verde Trail	Provided	526621	3558012	SW	Zylstra et al. 2006
P29	OCC	D	RMD	Mother's Day Fire Area	Provided	528513	3561369	SW	Zylstra et al. 2006
P30	OCC	D	RMD	Base of Rincons	Provided	530341	3564037	SW	Zylstra et al. 2006
P31	OCC	D	RMD	Cactus Forest Trail	Provided	525970	3560017	SW	Zylstra et al. 2006
P32	OCC	D	RMD	Mother's Day Fire Area	Provided	528058	3562202	SW	Zylstra et al. 2006
P33	OCC	D	RMD	Cactus Forest Trail	Provided	526276	3561413	SW	Zylstra et al. 2006
P38	OCC	D	RMD	Visitor Center	Provided	524753	3560591	SW	Zylstra et al. 2006
P39	OCC	D	RMD	Mother's Day Fire Area	Provided	528811	3562149	SW	Zylstra et al. 2006
P45	OCC	D	RMD	Javelina Picnic Area	Provided	526270	3558347	SW	Zylstra et al. 2006
P48	OCC	D	RMD	Cactus Forest Trail	Provided	525789	3559576	SW	Zylstra et al. 2006
P49	OCC	D	RMD	Wildhorse Canyon	Provided	529414	3563999	SW	Zylstra et al. 2006
T301	DS	D	TMD	GoldenGate/PictureRocks	Provided	484853	3575184	SW	SNP server
T302	DS	D	TMD	Sendero Esperanza Trail	Provided	484144	3571429	SW	SNP server
T304	DS	D	TMD	N of Wasson Peak	Provided	487218	3573264	SW	SNP server
T307	DS	D	TMD	Hugh Norris Trail	Provided	481670	3570476	SW	SNP server
T312	DS	D	TMD	Picture Rocks Rd	Provided	486819	3576042	SW	SNP server
T314	DS	D	TMD	N of Wasson Peak	Provided	485602	3572704	SW	SNP server
T316	DS	D	TMD	Sweetwater Trail	Provided	486858	3571459	SW	SNP server
T317	DS	D	TMD	N of Red Hills	Provided	483012	3569571	SW	SNP server
T322	DS	D	TMD	N of Wasson Peak	Provided	486045	3572391	SW	SNP server
T324	DS	D	TMD	Abington Rd	Provided	489371	3574830	SW	SNP server
T325	DS	D	TMD	Sendero Esperanza	Provided	484015	3570610	SW	SNP server

Transect/Plot ID	Type[a]	Project[b]	District[c]	General location	UTMs[d]	Easting[e]	Northing[e]	Corner[f]	Source of location info.[g]
T326	DS	D	TMD	Abington Rd	Provided	489612	3574559	SW	SNP server
T327	DS	D	TMD	Sandario Rd	Provided	479012	3570498	SW	SNP server
T328	DS	D	TMD	Gould Mine	Provided	484000	3568749	SW	SNP server
T331	DS	D	TMD	End of Sweetwater Rd	Provided	488304	3569336	SW	SNP server
T333	DS	D	TMD	Panther Peak	Provided	484305	3577145	SW	SNP server
T335	DS	D	TMD	Dobe Wash	Provided	483484	3571578	SW	SNP server
T336	DS	D	TMD	Dobe Wash	Provided	480837	3569582	SW	SNP server
T337	DS	D	TMD	GoldenGate/PictureRocks	Provided	484962	3576349	SW	SNP server
T339	DS	D	TMD	N of Ez-Kim-In-Zin	Provided	483251	3573929	SW	SNP server
T340	DS	D	TMD	N of Wasson Peak	Provided	485227	3572212	SW	SNP server
T343	DS	D	TMD	N of Red Hills	Provided	483234	3569432	SW	SNP server
T346	DS	D	TMD	SW of Contzen Pass	Provided	487391	3575683	SW	SNP server
T355	DS	D	TMD	N of Sus Picnic Area	Provided	480761	3571285	SW	SNP server
T359	DS	D	TMD	N of Ez-Kim-In-Zin	Provided	482849	3573615	SW	SNP server
T365	DS	D	TMD	N of Wasson Peak	Provided	485417	3572101	SW	SNP server
T366	DS	D	TMD	Panther Peak	Provided	483407	3578043	SW	SNP server
T367	DS	D	TMD	N of Ez-Kim-In-Zin	Provided	483881	3572499	SW	SNP server
T368	DS	D	TMD	Sweetwater Trail	Provided	486302	3571335	SW	SNP server
T370	DS	D	TMD	Sweetwater Trail	Provided	487333	3571649	SW	SNP server
T371	DS	D	TMD	Apache Peak	Provided	481478	3572589	SW	SNP server
T373	DS	D	TMD	GoldenGate/PictureRocks	Provided	486072	3575953	SW	SNP server
T375	DS	D	TMD	Panther Peak	Provided	485277	3577364	SW	SNP server
T376	DS	D	TMD	N of Ez-Kim-In-Zin	Provided	483479	3573238	SW	SNP server
T383	DS	D	TMD	Lower King Canyon	Provided	485396	3568364	SW	SNP server
T385	DS	D	TMD	Hugh Norris Area	Provided	480536	3569967	SW	SNP server
T390	DS	D	TMD	Apache Peak	Provided	482177	3572457	SW	SNP server
T393	DS	D	TMD	End of Sweetwater Rd	Provided	487707	3570137	SW	SNP server
T397	DS	D	TMD	Belmont Rd	Provided	491151	3575968	SW	SNP server
T399	DS	D	TMD	Panther Peak	Provided	484579	3577443	SW	SNP server
T407	DS	D	TMD	N of Ez-Kim-In-Zin	Provided	483957	3572889	SW	SNP server
T408	DS	D	TMD	Safford Peak	Provided	486507	3578577	SW	SNP server
T409	DS	D	TMD	Red Hills	Provided	483045	3568695	SW	SNP server
T411	DS	D	TMD	GoldenGate/PictureRocks	Provided	486054	3575182	SW	SNP server
T412	DS	D	TMD	W of Panther Peak	Provided	482943	3578999	SW	SNP server
T418	DS	D	TMD	N of Ez-Kim-In-Zin	Provided	482229	3573492	SW	SNP server

Transect/Plot ID	Type[a]	Project[b]	District[c]	General location	UTMs[d]	Easting[e]	Northing[e]	Corner[f]	Source of location info.[g]
T419	DS	D	TMD	N of Sus Picnic Area	Provided	480782	3571023	SW	SNP server
T421	DS	D	TMD	Panther Peak	Provided	483913	3578152	SW	SNP server
T422	DS	D	TMD	GoldenGate/PictureRocks	Provided	485923	3575424	SW	SNP server
T424	DS	D	TMD	Upper King Canyon	Provided	486335	3568913	SW	SNP server
T431	DS	D	TMD	N of Ez-Kim-In-Zin	Provided	482739	3573372	SW	SNP server
T433	DS	D	TMD	N of Wasson Peak	Provided	486114	3572948	SW	SNP server
T447	DS	D	TMD	Sendero Esperanza	Provided	483767	3570085	SW	SNP server
T450	DS	D	TMD	N of Hugh Norris	Provided	482189	3570969	SW	SNP server
T455	DS	D	TMD	Hugh Norris Trail	Provided	481053	3570479	SW	SNP server
T468	DS	D	TMD	Golden Gate Rd	Provided	485614	3574348	SW	SNP server
T469	DS	D	TMD	GoldenGate/PictureRocks	Provided	485981	3575723	SW	SNP server
T475	DS	D	TMD	Gould Mine	Provided	484637	3569005	SW	SNP server
T477	DS	D	TMD	Apache Peak	Provided	481888	3572553	SW	SNP server
T483	DS	D	TMD	N of Red Hills	Provided	482555	3569430	SW	SNP server
P101	OCC	D	TMD	Abington Rd	Provided	490103	3575434	SW	SNP server
P104	OCC	D	TMD	N of Red Hills	Provided	482564	3569200	SW	SNP server
P105	OCC	D	TMD	N of Ez-Kim-In-Zin	Provided	483009	3573328	SW	SNP server
P109	OCC	D	TMD	W of Panther Peak	Provided	483370	3578331	SW	SNP server
P117	OCC	D	TMD	N of Wasson Peak	Provided	486973	3573214	SW	SNP server
P118	OCC	D	TMD	N of Ez-Kim-In-Zin	Provided	483803	3573377	SW	SNP server
P119	OCC	D	TMD	Upper King Canyon	Provided	485563	3569351	SW	SNP server
P123	OCC	D	TMD	N of Ez-Kim-In-Zin	Provided	483136	3572589	SW	SNP server
P126	OCC	D	TMD	Gila Monster Mine	Provided	488850	3573536	SW	SNP server
P127	OCC	D	TMD	W of Panther Peak	Provided	483695	3578807	SW	SNP server
P130	OCC	D	TMD	Rudasill Rd	Provided	482361	3574081	SW	SNP server
P133	OCC	D	TMD	Golden Gate Rd	Provided	485472	3572402	SW	SNP server
P134	OCC	D	TMD	Sendero Esperanza	Provided	482965	3570245	SW	SNP server
P141	OCC	D	TMD	End of Sweetwater Rd	Provided	488606	3570117	SW	SNP server
P146	OCC	D	TMD	Sendero Esperanza	Provided	483849	3571364	SW	SNP server
P148	OCC	D	TMD	Contzen Pass	Provided	487423	3576370	SW	SNP server
P152	OCC	D	TMD	King Canyon	Provided	484354	3568199	SW	SNP server
P153	OCC	D	TMD	S of Contzen Pass	Provided	487281	3575464	SW	SNP server
P155	OCC	D	TMD	Sendero Esperanza	Provided	483362	3570138	SW	SNP server
P158	OCC	D	TMD	Contzen Pass	Provided	488140	3576817	SW	SNP server

[a]Type: DS = distance-sampling transect, MR = mark-recapture plot, OCC = occupancy site, VET = visual encounter transect.

[b]Project: A = Goldsmith-Shaw population studies 1988-1990, B = Wirt-Lowe population studies 1995-1998, C = Urban impact studies 1999-2001, D = Zylstra-Steidl monitoring study 2005-2006.

[c]District: RMD = Rincon Mountain District, TMD= Tucson Mountain District.

[d]UTMs: Approx. = Approximated UTMs from plot boundaries drawn on topographic maps, Provided = UTMs provided in a report or electronic file associated with the study, Unavailable = UTMs unavailable.

[e]Easting and Northing: all locations provided in NAD83 datum.

[f]Corner: Specifies which of the four corner locations the provided UTMs describe for distance-sampling transects, mark-recapture plots, and occupancy sites that were laid out as rectangles or squares along the cardinal directions. All distance-sampling transects were laid out as 250 m x 250 m squares; all occupancy sites were laid out as 170 m x 170 m squares. Locations of the NW, NE, and SE corners of distance-sampling transects and occupancy sites were not provided as locations could be extrapolated from locations of the SW corners.

[g]Source of location info.: Source of transect or plot location information. Wirt maps = set of topographic maps with hand-drawn transect locations provided to Saguaro National Park by Betsy Wirt and stored at the Saguaro National Park resource office, Misc. project materials = miscellaneous project information and data sheets provided by Audrey Goldsmith to Saguaro National Park and stored at WACC, Saguaro National Park Server = electronic files with survey locations provided by principal investigator to the park and stored on the N: drive of the Saguaro National Park server.

Appendix B. Notching systems used for desert tortoises at Saguaro National Park.

Wirt 1996 System

Used to mark tortoises throughout Saguaro National Park from 1988-present except where noted below.

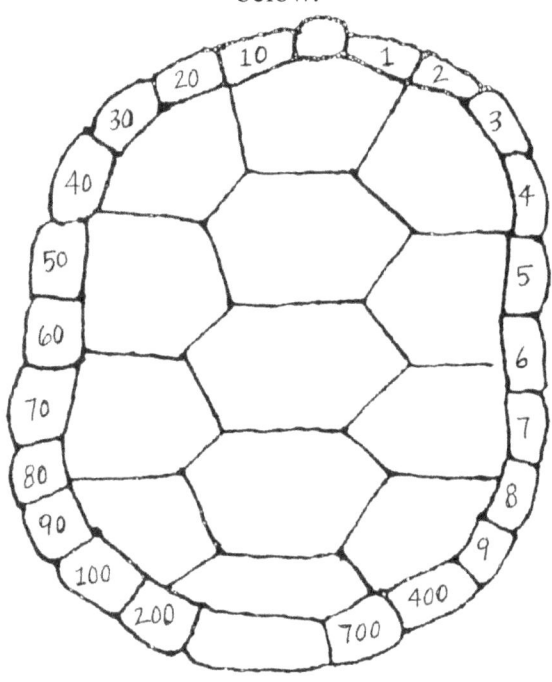

Arizona (Rocking K) System

Used to mark tortoises in the Rocking-K Ranch-Saguaro National Park Expansion area from 1999-present

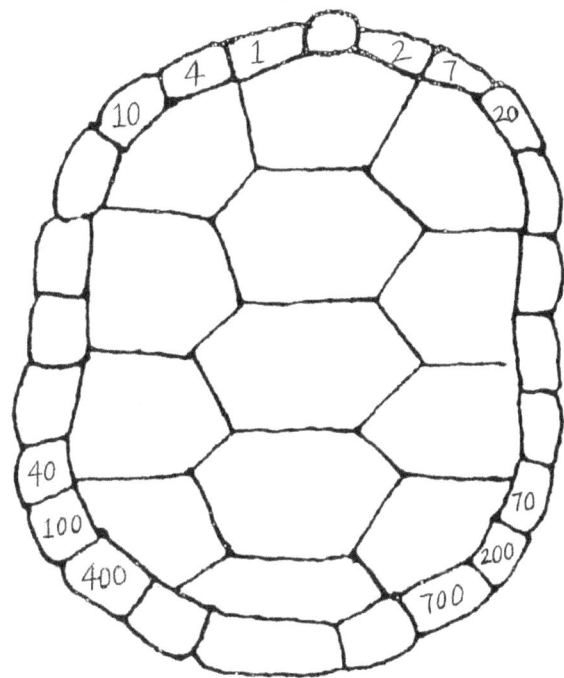

Cagle 1939 System
Used to mark tortoises in the Mother's Day Fire area from 1994-1995

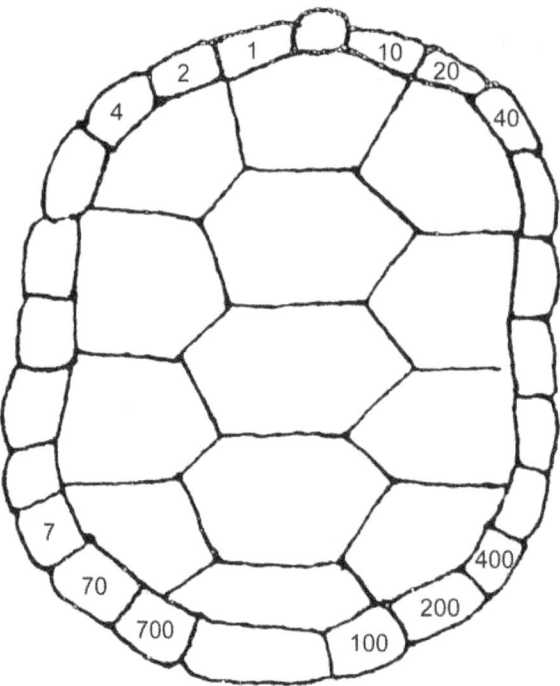

NPS D-183, April 2009

National Park Service
U.S. Department of the Interior

Natural Resource Program Center
1201 Oakridge Drive, Suite 150
Fort Collins, CO 80525

www.nature.nps.gov

www.ingramcontent.com/pod-product-compliance
Lightning Source LLC
Chambersburg PA
CBHW080916290526
45795CB00007BA/2539